THE OUTDOOR CHUMS ON THE GULF

Or

Rescuing the Lost Balloonists

Captain Quincy Allen

1st WORLD LIBRARY Literary Society

The Outdoor Chums on the Gulf

Captain Quincy Allen

© 1st World Library, 2006
PO Box 2211
Fairfield, IA 52556
www.1stworldlibrary.com
First Edition

LCCN: 2006907727

Softcover ISBN: 1-4218-2450-7
Hardcover ISBN: 1-4218-2350-0
eBook ISBN: 1-4218-2550-3

Purchase *"The Outdoor Chums on the Gulf"*
as a traditional bound book at:
www.1stWorldLibrary.com/purchase.asp?ISBN=1-4218-2450-7

1st World Library is a literary, educational organization
dedicated to:

- Creating a free internet library of downloadable ebooks

- Hosting writing competitions and offering book
publishing scholarships.

Interested in more 1st World Library books?
contact: literacy@1stworldlibrary.com
Check us out at: www.1stworldlibrary.com

1ˢᵗ World Library Literary Society

Giving Back to the World

"If you want to work on the core problem, it's early school literacy."

- James Barksdale, former CEO of Netscape

"No skill is more crucial to the future of a child, or to a democratic and prosperous society, than literacy."

- Los Angeles Times

Literacy... means far more than learning how to read and write... The aim is to transmit... knowledge and promote social participation."

- UNESCO

"Literacy is not a luxury, it is a right and a responsibility. If our world is to meet the challenges of the twenty-first century we must harness the energy and creativity of all our citizens."

- President Bill Clinton

"Parents should be encouraged to read to their children, and teachers should be equipped with all available techniques for teaching literacy, so the varying needs and capacities of individual kids can be taken into account."

- Hugh Mackay

CONTENTS

I. UNDER SEALED ORDERS 9

II. CAUGHT IN A FIRE TRAP 17

III. HEADED SOUTH 24

IV. JERRY MEETS TROUBLE HALF WAY 30

V. THE FIRST CAMPFIRE 36

VI. THE SWAMP FUGITIVE 43

VII. A FLORIDA SHERIFF 51

VIII. WILL DOES IT 58

IX .THE MOTOR-BOAT AND THE PROWLERS 63

X. BLUFF'S FIRST 'GATOR 71

XI. ALL THE COMFORTS OF SALT WATER 78

XII. THE BREAKDOWN OF THE MOTOR 85

XIII. LOST IN THE FOG 92

XIV. A CRY ACROSS THE LAGOON 99

XV. A VISIT TO THE MYSTERIOUS SHARPIE 107

XVI. JOE 114

XVII. STUCK ON AN OYSTER BAR 121

XVIII. TROUBLE 128

XIX. WHAT HAPPENED TO JERRY 135

XX. LYING IN AMBUSH FOR BIG GAME 143

XXI. A STRENUOUS NIGHT 150

XXII. THE MESSAGE FROM THE AIR 158

XXIII. A DASH UPON THE GULF 165

XXIV. THE "NORTHER" 174

XXV. THE SECRET OF THE SEALED PACKET
    - CONCLUSION 181

CHAPTER I

UNDER SEALED ORDERS

"Now KEEP your word, Frank, and tell us the news!"

"Yes, you got us to come to your house tonight under a promise, remember. What wonderful thing has happened to make you look so tickled?"

"Talk to me about the Sphinx! Frank has the old relic beaten to a frazzle!"

Three boys gathered eagerly around the fourth as they bombarded him after this fashion. Frank Langdon looked at the faces of his chums and laughed again.

"Well, it would be a shame to keep you squirming on the anxious seat any longer, boys, and I'm going to take you into my confidence just as fast as I can. Sit down and hold your oars. Jerry, pull that stool up; Will, the settee must do for you and Bluff. Now, are you ready?" he asked, tantalizingly.

"Crazy to hear!" was the characteristic reply of Bluff, otherwise Richard Masters, son of Centerville's greatest lawyer.

"Tell me about that, will you?" exclaimed Jerry Wallington.

"Please go on before we explode!" begged Will Milton.

"These things always have a beginning, you know. This one happens to be founded on the fact that we are close to our annual Christmas vacation, and that this year it happens that we're going to enjoy two full weeks - you know that?" said Frank.

"Of course we do, thanks to that steam-heater getting out of order. But don't rehash old stuff. That's history by now. What we want is the meat in the cocoanut. Please hit for the bull's-eye, first chop," pleaded Will.

"I was wondering what we would do with ourselves during that time. There's old Jesse Wilcox, the trapper, who invited us up to spend a week with him and see how he runs out his string of traps in cold weather, catching muskrats, mink, 'coons, foxes and all such things in more or less abundance. We had about decided that we would accept, and I was even getting ready to go when something happened."

"Talk to me about your tantalizing chaps, did you ever meet up with one as bad as Frank can be when he knows the rest of us are so keen to hear?" cried Jerry.

"What was it?" demanded Bluff.

"I had a letter that changed my mind," replied Frank.

"Not from old Jesse?"

"Well, hardly, for I don't believe the old fellow can write. This was from one of my cousins, a fellow several years older than myself. You met him about a year ago when he stopped with us a few days."

"You must mean Archie Dunn," said Will.

"Go up head, Will. Archie it was. I was glad enough to get a letter from him, but when I read what he had to propose I thought I should have a fit."

"Just as we will, unless you hurry your yarn," growled Jerry, moving uneasily.

"Well, Archie wrote that he had laid out a plan for his amusement this winter. You know he is independent, having come into quite a snug fortune. He is as fond of outdoor life as any member of this club, and, having a tutor to accompany him, is able to do lots of splendid stunts that less fortunate chaps can only dream about."

"The lucky dog!" commented Bluff, enviously.

"It seems that this year he was about to carry out a long-cherished plan of his. He purchased a beautiful little motor-boat, about twenty-seven feet long, and carrying a twelve horse-power engine. He says she can make twelve miles an hour if pushed, but being beamy she is as steady as a church floor and mighty comfortable; just the kind of a craft for cruising along a river or the bays of a coast."

Jerry groaned.

"You're killing me by inches! To tell us all this and then ask us to settle on going up there into the woods for a two-weeks' spin! It's a crime, that's what!" he exclaimed.

"Wait!" said Frank, mysteriously; and the others immediately drew a bit closer, almost holding their very breath with eagerness and anticipation.

"He had this boat taken to a Southern town on the railroad, where a navigable river flows through Northern Florida into the Gulf. Here he also shipped all his provisions, intending to make a start just before Christmas, when the unexpected happened. He had an accident - broke through the ice when skating, came near being drowned, and has been laid up with pneumonia ever since!"

"Poor chap! That's awful!" declared Bluff.

"But that isn't the worst by any means, from our standpoint, boys. His doctor has strictly forbidden him to take that voyage this winter and is sending him off with his tutor to some baths in Southern Europe or some old place where he may recover his strength."

The three boys groaned in concert.

"A rough deal all around," said Jerry.

"What a disappointment it must have been, and he with his heart set on the trip!" exclaimed Will.

"But they tell us that 'it's a poor wind that blows nobody good.' So he has written me this letter, making a proposal," went on Frank, calmly.

"What!" shouted Jerry, clutching the arm of his chum.

"Oh! he hates to leave his fine, dandy little launch there at that town, where there is really no accommodation for her, and would like to have some one take her over the course to Cedar Keys, Florida, to put her up with a boat builder he knows. And so he wrote to me," continued Frank.

"Do you mean he has asked you to go down there and take that boat, just as he intended doing?" gasped Bluff.

"Yes, only that instead of taking two months loitering along I could do the job in ten days, perhaps," was the answer.

"Oh! what a lucky dog you are," sighed Will; "think of the innumerable chances for taking magnificent snapshots along the way."

"Hold on. I didn't tell you that in his letter he says particularly, 'you and those bully good chums of yours, the whole three - plenty of sleeping accommodations for the lot aboard!'" cried Frank, with a smile.

Then there *was* a scene! Jerry gripped Bluff, and gave him a hug a bear might have envied, while Will was shaking Frank's hand as though it were a pump handle.

"Glorious!"

"The finest ever!"

"It beats the Dutch how Frank runs into snaps!"

This last, of course, from Jerry, who was taking his turn now at squeezing the hand of his chum.

"But, I'm afraid, fellows, that we won't ever get the consent of our parents," sighed Will. "My mother would hate to have me go so far away. You know she only has my twin sister Violet and myself. Oh! it's sure too good to be true."

"Now don't cross a river until you come to it, fellows. To tell you the truth, that part of the programme has already been attended to. My father and myself have been the rounds unbeknown to any of you, and got the consent of Will's mother, as well as the parents of Bluff and Jerry. It's a settled thing, boys!"

They sat there and stared at each other. Evidently none of them could fully grasp the wonderful proposition entirely. They thought they must be dreaming.

"Please don't wake me up; this is too bang-up for anything," said Will.

"Frank, your equal never existed. Talk to me about your chums, no fellows ever had such a boss comrade as your fellow-members of the Rod, Gun and Camera Club!" declared Jerry.

"When do we start?" demanded Bluff, as though ready to run for the train at that very minute.

"The day after to-morrow. School closes in one more day, and father thought it wouldn't matter much if we slipped off a bit ahead of time. He will fix it with the Head all right. So, now you've got to be as busy as bees getting your duffle in readiness between now and the time the train goes, eight A.M. sharp."

"That governor of yours is certainly the finest ever. How did it come that he fell in with the idea so quickly? Did you have to beg hard?" asked Will.

"That's the strangest part of it, as I'll tell you presently. He fairly jumped at the idea when I told him about Cedar Keys. But we must spend the whole evening settling just what we are to take along with us," ventured Frank.

"What did you say about grub?" queried Bluff, whose appetite never failed him.

"Archie wants us to accept all he has laid in, and encloses the list. I need add only a few little things that I happen to know one or the other of us fancies especially, and we are fixed for two weeks. You see there were two of them, and they expected to be afloat two months, so he laid in a large quantity of bacon, coffee, tea, sugar, and all substantials, much more than we can ever use; and I know Archie well enough to make sure they came from the best grocery in New York."

"Oh! the darling, won't we remember him in our prayers, boys, and hope he gets good and strong over at that cure in Europe? There will be never a meal but that our thanks will ascend for this good deed of Cousin Archie. He belongs to all of us; this club adopts him as its one honorary member; and I hereby propose three cheers for the biggest-hearted chap going. Hip, hip, hurray!"

Doubtless Frank's father and mother exchanged smiles when this hearty cheer came to their ears from Frank's den; but Mr. Langdon, even though a staid banker now, never forgot that he had once been a boy himself; and they understood the enthusiasm that must inevitably sweep over the three chums of Frank when they heard the glorious news.

So the boys proceeded to go into executive session, and jot down lists of such things as they would be apt to need on the outing.

"I understand that Archie had some heavy fishing tackle in his supplies, which we can count on to carry us through. Take your heavy rods only, and your guns, with proper ammunition," suggested Frank.

"And I'll lay in a stock of films and such things, for I expect to get lots of fine pictures among those wonderful Southern scenes. I've always wanted to see that Spanish moss trailing from the swamp trees like it is in all Southern views. I'm the happiest chap in Centerville tonight, Frank!" exclaimed Will.

"But see here," interrupted Bluff, "how about that matter connected with your good dad, Frank - why was he so pleased at the idea of you going to Cedar Keys?"

"Yes, tell us about that," burst out Jerry.

"It's a big mystery, fellows. Father smiled and nodded his head when I read him Archie's letter. 'What a remarkable coincidence. I was just thinking of going to that city myself, or sending a trusted messenger, and now you can do it all for me,' he said."

The boys exchanged looks.

"Don't it just beat all?" remarked Jerry, weakly.

"Why, we're having the luckiest streak of our lives, that's what. But see here, Frank, didn't he tell you more?" remarked Bluff, who always wanted to know, being the son of a lawyer.

"He gave me this little packet, done up in a stout manila

envelope, and told me not to open it until I came in sight of Cedar Keys. Inside would be found full instructions as to what errand he wanted me to carry out."

"Better and better! We sail under sealed orders, fellows. That should add a little zest to the voyage. I know I'll be consumed with curiosity every minute of the time wanting to know what under the sun it can be that your good dad has waiting for you to do," said Will, seriously.

"Well," remarked Frank, "you see me put the packet away, not to be opened until the proper time; and now we'd better go on with our lists."

CHAPTER II

CAUGHT IN A FIRE TRAP

It was late that night ere the three visitors thought of going home. There was so much to talk over that it seemed as though they could never break away.

"Listen!" exclaimed Will, finally, as they were about to depart.

"That's the fire-bell, as sure as you live!" cried Bluff.

"Tell me about that, will you!" cried Jerry. "A cold night to get burned out!"

Frank snatched up his coat and cap.

"I'm going with you, fellows, as far as the corner, anyway, and see if it is a real fire, or a fake," he remarked.

Accordingly the quartette rushed out of the door and down the street. There was snow on the ground, and the air was pretty keen.

"It's a fire all right; look, you can see the light, and the smoke!" said Will.

"Say, fellows, isn't that the square, and doesn't it look like it might be the Sherman House?" asked Frank.

"As sure as you live," replied Bluff. "That would be a tough thing, for the people there to climb out near midnight, and the mercury hovering half way down to zero!"

"Hurry! Perhaps we can help some!" exclaimed good-hearted Jerry, and they increased their pace.

It was the hotel, beyond all doubt. As the boys came into the open square they saw a scene of confusion that thrilled them. Smoke was pouring out of the lower windows of the big frame building, and in some places it was accompanied by red tongues of flame, licking up the dry wood.

"She's a goner!" announced Jerry grimly.

They saw people come hastily out of the doorway, some scantily clad, and with blankets around their shoulders. Luckily there were only a few guests in the hotel, since the best trade came in summer.

Loud shouts told that the local fire company was coming with their hand-engine. Probably the Chemical Company would also be on hand, although it was too late for anything to be done but try and save adjoining buildings, none of which, fortunately enough, were very close to the doomed hotel.

Frank and his chums thought that possibly they might help out at pumping, or doing something of the sort. At a fire in a country town every one assists to carry out furniture, or work the machine, while the regular members of the organization enjoy the exclusive privilege of carrying the hose and smashing in windows.

Amid the greatest excitement the water was finally started. By this time one end of the building was all on fire, and every person knew it would be a complete wreck before the flames ceased feeding.

It chanced that the boys were standing near some of those who had issued forth from the hotel. Among them was the proprietor, plainly excited as he saw his property going up in smoke and flames, and still getting some consolation from the fact that he had a good insurance on it all.

Just then a man came limping and seized hold of the hotel proprietor.

"Have you seen my brother, the professor?" he demanded, in a trembling voice.

"Oh! that you, Mr. Smythe? Your brother - no, I don't remember seeing him. But I guess everybody got out all right. He must be around somewhere," replied the other.

"I've asked a dozen people, and nobody has seen him. I tell you, man, he's asleep up in that room yet, and will be burned to death!" exclaimed the gentleman, whom Jerry knew quite well. He was very lame and walked with difficulty.

His brother, a balloonist of national reputation, had been visiting him recently, and on account of some sickness at the house, had taken a room at the hotel.

"But no sane man could sleep through all this beastly row; and sure we haven't seen any one at the windows, have we, boys?" went on the fat hotel man.

"But you don't understand. I tell you he has been unable to sleep for several nights, and just before he left me early to-night he took a sleeping powder that he said would make him dead to the world for eight hours! He's up in his room yet, and will be lost unless some one goes and drags him out!" cried Mr. Smythe.

"Which is his room, Mr. Ten Eyck?" demanded an eager voice.

The stout hotel man looked at the speaker, who was none

other than Jerry.

"You see that window over there at the end of the house, third floor - that's his room! But the stairs must be ablaze by now, boy! It would be suicide to think of trying to go up there!" he cried.

"Come on, Frank; we'll take a look in, anyhow!" shouted Jerry as he dashed off, followed by his chum, equally excited.

Still, Frank was ordinarily a cool-headed fellow, and accustomed to weighing chances somewhat before imperiling his life. In this case, of course, he knew that more or less risk must be taken if they hoped to save the sleeping balloonist.

One look they took in at the front door. The whole place was ablaze.

"Get out of the way, boys; we're going to put the hose in there!" cried one of the wearers of the fire-hats and coats, as he advanced.

"No chance there!" exclaimed Frank, in despair, as he moved back.

Jerry clutched his arm.

"Come along with me. Perhaps the back stairs may not be burning, yet. They happen to be further along toward the safe side. There's a chance!" he panted.

Half a minute later they had turned the corner, and were close to the rear exit.

"See, the smoke is coming out, but no fire. Shall we risk it?" asked the eager Jerry.

Frank swept a quick look above and around. He was weighing the thing in his mind, so that they might not be carried by impulse to their doom.

"It's worth while. At the worst we can jump into that tree from the window. And it's just terrible to think of the professor sleeping on until he is caught. Lead the way, Jerry; you know about it better than I do. Remember, on the third floor, and turn to the left!"

They darted in. Several persons near by shouted warnings, but the words fell on deaf ears, for already the daring lads were rushing up the narrow stairs. Around them the smoke was dense. It smarted their eyes dreadfully, so that they were compelled to rub them from time to time in order to see at all.

Reaching the first landing, Jerry turned to the left. Frank had hold of his chum's coat, for he did not want to get lost in that smoky interior, and Jerry was the one acquainted with the situation.

Now they had reached the second flight of stairs. A burst of red fire further along the hall served to show them for a brief space of time how matters stood. Up the stairs they stumbled, gaining the upper landing. Again Jerry turned to the left.

"He said the last room, didn't he?" he gasped.

"Yes, go on!" answered Frank, still gripping his comrade's garment.

"Then here's the door!"

"Shut?"

"Yes, and locked, too! What shall we do?" exclaimed Jerry.

"Kick it in - any old way, but we must be quick!" answered the other.

Then the two threw themselves upon the door. It quickly gave way before their combined assault. They pushed into the room. The smoke had gained a footing here, but on account of the closed door it was not nearly so bad as in the halls.

Immediately they saw a figure stretched across the bed. The balloonist had evidently been overcome by sleep before he thought to undress, and dropped over just as he had come from his lame brother's house.

"Wake up, professor, the house is on fire!" shouted Frank in the ear of the man.

Jerry, meanwhile, was shaking him vigorously; but all their efforts seemed to be of no avail. The man slept on as peacefully as though a babe, such was the power of the drug he had taken.

"We can't stay here long," said Frank, as the smoke thickened in the room. "And as he won't wake up, why, we'll have to try and carry or drag him down."

Fortunately, the man was not a very large person, or they might have despaired of ever accomplishing such a thing.

"Take hold on that side, Jerry. Now, lift, and drag his heels. That's the only way we can do," exclaimed Frank, who feared that even short as their stay in that room had been they would find conditions changed for the worse when they again reached the hall.

The professor paid not the least attention to what they were doing. He had possibly taken an overdose of his sleeping-powder, and only for the coming of the two chums must have perished miserably, like a rat in a trap.

When Frank threw open the door of the room again he uttered a cry of alarm. The back stairway was a mass of flame. Although hardly more than two minutes had passed since they came up those stairs, it was now manifestly impossible to pass down again.

He slammed the door shut and found Jerry staring at him in the half light.

"Talk to me about your fiery furnaces, that beats them all!" exclaimed Frank's chum, as he let go the professor's shoulders. "What shall we do now?"

Frank ran over to the window and threw up the sash. He looked out and then came back to where Jerry stood, trembling with excitement. Frank was as cool as ever in his life.

"There's a chance, Jerry," he shouted. "No fire below! Take hold here; tear up these sheets and knot them into a rope. Work for your life, and if the fire only holds back we may be able to save both the professor and ourselves! But work! work!"

CHAPTER III

HEADED SOUTH

They did work with a vim, for the smoke was getting more oppressive with each passing second; and from the glimpse they had taken of the stairway it was plain to the boys that presently the fire would wrap the whole south end of the building in its grip, when their case would indeed be desperate.

Each tore and knotted until as if by magic a long rope was fashioned. True, it might betray them at the last and break, but Frank believed the sheets to be of good material and nearly new.

He had not time to even test the frail rope, but fastened it around the sleeping balloonist, under his arms.

"Now help me lift him over the window-sill," he cried.

They had little difficulty in doing that, for the professor was a small, slight man. Once he was passed over the ledge, they began to lower away.

Frank only hoped in his heart that the fire might restrain its fury for a brief space of time. If it darted out below it must catch the human burden which they were lowering so speedily.

Shouts were heard outside. It seemed as though fully an hundred voices were raised to applaud the daring feat of the

Captain Quincy Allen

two boys, as the figure of the professor was seen coming rapidly down at the end of the rope made of torn sheets.

"If it's only long enough!" gasped Jerry.

"Hurrah! they've got hold of him! He's saved!" roared Frank, as the tremendous pull suddenly ceased.

They had about reached the end of the rope, so that this happy event came just in the nick of time. Frank hurriedly fastened that end to the bed-post.

"Climb out, Jerry, and slide down. Not a word now, or we may lose our chance!"

Jerry had been about to object, wishing his chum to go first. He realized the truth of what Frank said, however, and how foolish it would be to stand back on a matter so small. Accordingly he clambered over the window-sill and vanished from view.

Frank got in position to follow, and only waited until he had reason to believe his chum had reached safety. The rope had done bravely, but it certainly could never stand the strain of two of them at the same time.

And even as he waited there was a flash of fire below, as the flames ate through the sheathing of the house. A tremendous yell went up.

"Come down, Frank - oh! quick!" he caught above the clamor, and he knew that it was Will's shrill voice he heard.

The fire was perilously close to the rope. In a second it might catch and be severed. Frank did not hesitate. He was accustomed to meeting emergencies promptly, and doing the right thing.

Down he slipped, passing the threatening flame, in fact

shooting through it just as the rope began to be consumed in its hot breath. Frank had almost reached the point of safety when he felt his support collapse, and he dropped downward.

Something caught him, something that seemed endowed with life - the extended arms of his three chums eagerly fashioned into a net, and he was not injured, beyond a little singeing of his hair as he passed through the fiery torch.

The boys were glad to get away from the crowd of enthusiastic admirers who wanted to lift Frank and Jerry on their shoulders, and carry them around town in triumph, something that felt repulsive to the lads.

But the lame brother of the man they had saved, seized upon them ere they went off.

"A thousand thanks to you, for your brave deed!" he cried. "You have saved a human life to-night, boys, and one of more than ordinary value. My brother is employed by the Government to experiment with balloons and aeroplanes, and his discoveries may prove a great thing for our nation in case of a foreign war. To-morrow he will thank you himself, and from his heart. Your mothers have cause to be proud of their sons, and I shall tell them so myself."

From a distance the boys watched the hotel burn, and talked over the affair just as though they might have been casual watchers, and had no particular interest in the matter. And yet two of them had come very close to sacrificing their young lives in attempting to save that of another.

Both Bluff and Will had suffered tortures while their chums were inside the doomed structure. Their voices had led all the rest as the sheet-rope fell from the upper window, with the form of the professor dangling at the end, for they knew the daring plan of their mates had been a brilliant success.

The fire did not jump to any of the nearby dwellings or stores, thanks to the efficient labors of the department, the members of which worked like Trojans in order to confine it to its original field.

When it had died down the boys separated once more, and the hearty grip that passed between them was evidence of the sincere affection that bound this quartette of clean, manly fellows in common.

Neither Frank nor Jerry said a word to their parents about the heroic part they had played in the rescue of Professor Smythe. Imagine the astonishment of Frank's father when that gentleman, in company with his brother, a respected business man of Centerville, called at the house, the next morning after breakfast, and related the whole circumstance.

And when Frank and Jerry were called down from the den, where, in company with the others, they were doing some packing, they blushed under the hearty words of praise heaped upon them by the two gentlemen.

"Why, I'm going South myself, boys," declared the balloonist, when he heard of their contemplated trip, "and wouldn't it be a queer thing now if we happened to come across one another down in Dixieland? I'm heading for Atlanta, to steer my big balloon to the eastward at the first favorable chance, in order to settle some questions about air currents that have long been baffling us all. Depend on it, if I could do you any sort of a favor I'd go far out of my way to try and even up the debt I owe you."

Little did any of them suspect under what strange conditions their next meeting would really be.

All Centerville was ringing with the story of the brave exploit of Frank and Jerry. When the latter reached home that noon he was overwhelmed with hysterical words of praise from his mother; while his father had come home from his office, beset by a dozen acquaintances desirous of congratulating him on having a son of such heroic mould.

Jerry was very uneasy under all this favorable comment. He did not like to be looked upon as differing in any degree from other boys.

"Any fellow would have done the same thing. We were lucky enough to have the chance, that's all," he insisted, as his mother kissed him again and again, crying a little at the same time at the thought of what might have happened; while his father gripped his hand and patted him on the back affectionately.

By afternoon the boys decided that they had everything packed they could think of, and after that they began to try and possess their souls in patience.

"No sleep for me to-night, fellows," declared Jerry, as he prepared to go home, as supper-time came around.

"I'd advise you to try and get a few winks if you can. To-morrow night we'll be on the train, and not much chance then. It's a lucky thing that all of us know something about machinery. Our experience with our motor-cycles will come in good play now. And here's Jerry been studying up on the running of an automobile with that retired chauffeur, Garrison, who's teaching Andy Lasher how to run a car."

"Yes, but, Frank, how about you taking lessons about the engine of a motor-boat? I know you've got several books on the subject since your father half promised to put a little craft on Lake Camalot next season," remarked Jerry.

"Well," laughed Frank, fairly caught, "between the lot of us it'll be strange if we don't know how to handle that dandy boat of Cousin Archie's - the *Jessamine* he calls her."

"Three cheers for the *Jessamine*, then!" said Bluff.

They were given with a will, after which the boys separated. Since this would be their last night at home for two weeks they had sensibly decided to spend it in the bosom of their families. Everything was done, at any rate, so that it was useless to bother about that matter any more.

In spite of Frank's warning it is very unlikely that any one of the four slept very soundly. The near future beckoned to them with such grand possibilities concerning the sport they loved, that they could not get it out of their minds; and innumerable plans for the happy times ahead kept their brains busy the major portion of that last night under the parental roof-trees.

Finally the morning dawned, with a light snow falling. There was a bustle in at least four homes that day, and presently the intending travelers gathered at the station long before the train was due that would take them on to Philadelphia, and then, with a change of cars, to the beckoning sunny Southland.

And when finally the parting moment came, there were hurried good-byes, the bags were thrown into the baggage car, and as the train pulled out those of their school friends who had come down to see them off, as well as their relatives, waved a shower of handkerchiefs amid a chorus of shouts.

"Hurrah!" cried Bluff, as he settled down in his seat, "we're on the way to the greatest time of our lives!"'

CHAPTER IV

JERRY MEETS TROUBLE HALF WAY

"Ain't she a beauty, though?"

"Finest thing ever put in the water! And to think we're going to live aboard her for nearly two weeks! It's the greatest luck ever!" observed Will.

"Talk to me about your automobiles and aeroplanes, give me a neat little motor-boat for mine. I wouldn't change places with King George just now."

Frank said nothing, but the smile on his face was a satisfied one. Indeed, it could not well be otherwise. Any boy who loved camping and cruising as much as he did must have been thrilled at the prospect of running that jaunty little craft for a spell, navigating new waterways and making discoveries constantly, such as are calculated to please the hearts of hunters and water-dogs in general.

The motor-boat was one of the most modern make. It had an automobile hood for the front, and this could be so extended that the entire boat was shielded. On the other hand, on sunny days it could be pushed back, allowing of perfect freedom.

The journey south had been effected without any accident. They were now stopping at a little hotel in this town on the river where the railroad crossed. It was a section of Northern

Florida. The great and mysterious Gulf of Mexico, they knew, lay not a far stretch away toward the south. Indeed, Jerry had declared he could already smell salt water, though his chums laughed at him, and declared that it was more likely the odor of the mud along the bank of the narrow but deep stream down which they expected to cruise shortly.

"All the same, I'll be mighty glad to set eyes on that same gulf," said Jerry; "I've always wanted to see it, ever since I read about the doings of those old filibusters who used to lie in wait and seize the treasure ships going home from the Spanish Main."

"Listen to him, will you?" broke out Bluff, laughing. "Honest, now, I believe he expects to run across a few of those old fossil pirates, Blackbeard, Captain Kidd and their kind."

"Well, hardly, but it may be we'll meet up with a few up-to-date pirates before we get through - chaps who can charge ten prices for something you just feel you must have. The times are out of joint, boys. Things have changed a little, that's all, but the world is just as full of human sharks as ever," argued Jerry.

"I guess Jerry's right, fellows, and when that gaunt landlord of the inn presents his little bill perhaps you'll say that the buccaneer came sooner than you expected. Besides, who can say what lies before us? There are many swamps to be passed through, I'm told, and they say that more than one fugitive black, wanted for some crime, lives out in those places. We must keep our eyes open all the time."

"And depend on it, Frank knows. He's been picking up information right and left ever since we got here," remarked Will, who was, of course, carrying his beloved camera, with which he had taken many splendid pictures of the past exploits of the four chums.

"When do we get under way?" asked Bluff, eagerly, as he examined the provisions made for cooking, with a battery of little lamps fashioned to burn kerosene in the shape of gas - Bluff was always interested in all that pertained to the cooking parts of an expedition.

"Everything is ready now," remarked Frank. "We'll go back to the inn, all but Will, settle our score, and fetch what few things are left. I've got a rough chart of the river, you know, boys, on which we'll have to depend until we get to the gulf."

"And then?" asked Will.

"Oh, the Government charts will carry us, then, the rest of the way. They have everything down, up to several miles off shore, and all the bayous and cuts besides. Come on, Jerry and Bluff; get busy."

Left in charge of the boat for half an hour, Will sat there in the warm sunshine, trying to picture what it looked like up around cold, bleak Centerville just then. As he fondled his camera other memories were called up, in which it had done its share in the way of perpetuating the exciting events connected with the various outings enjoyed by the four chums.

While Will sits thus and lets his mind wander back to other scenes it may be just as well for us to take a quick survey of these same events, so as to understand something of the ties that held these four boys together.

They formed the Rod, Gun and Camera Club, and their first outing had been at the time a storm took part of the Academy roof off, allowing a short Fall vacation on the part of the scholars. At that time they had gone into the woods, and there encountered a variety of stirring adventures, as set forth in the initial volume of this series called: "The Outdoor Chums; or, The First Tour of the Rod, Gun and Camera Club."

At Thanksgiving time they planned for another little camping trip, over on Wildcat Island, which had quite a bad name on account of the ferocious animals known to exist in its dense thickets, and also because a wild man was said to have been seen there many times. What the four chums saw and did there, and the multitude of remarkable things that came to pass while they were off on this trip, from the robbery on the steamboat to the discovery about the wild man, are told in the second book of the series, entitled: "The Outdoor Chums on the Lake; or, Lively Adventures on Wildcat Island,"

In due time came the summer vacation, and as they had a couple of weeks to be together before going away to seashore or mountains with their parents, the boys arranged to spend this time in the Sunset Mountains, that lay ten miles back of Newtonport, which place was on the west shore of the lake, opposite Centerville. The rumor of a ghost that was said to haunt Oak Ridge did much to draw the boys, and it can be readily understood that before they left their camp in the hills they had succeeded in discovering the astonishing truth about that same spectre. Just how this was done, together with many other thrilling episodes, you will find in the record of the outing as given in the third volume, called: "The Outdoor Chums in the Forest; or, Laying the Ghost of Oak Ridge."

By the time Will had run the gamut of these adventures, some of which caused him to shiver, while others brought a smile on his face, he heard the voices of his chums drawing near.

They soon joined him, each burdened with some more of the outfit in the way of blankets, and clothes-bags made of waterproof canvas.

These were hastily stowed away, after which the boys began to get busy. Frank had, ere now, closely examined the engine of the launch, and even started it going so as to get "the hang of the thing," as he said. He felt that he had nothing to fear with regard to his ability to handle it.

"If anything does happen we will have to use the push-poles, and in that way float down on the swift current until we get to a town," he said, laughingly; but not one of them had the slightest fear.

"All aboard for the gulf!" called Will, as he stood by the rail watching Jerry unwarp the hawser that held the nose of the boat down-stream, another securing the stern above.

Just as soon as this latter was unfastened the boat would begin to move with the rapid current, and at that time Frank wanted his engine to be working.

"Ready, Frank?" called Jerry from astern.

He could cast off there, recovering the rope as they moved along.

The engine began to whirr.

"Say, doesn't that sound encouraging?" ventured Bluff, as the cheery cough smote the air, and announced the whole power of twelve horses to be at their disposal.

"I only hope she turns out one-half as good as she looks," remarked Frank, who believed that the proof of the pudding lay in the eating of it.

A minute later, satisfied that everything was working, he shouted:

"Let her go, Jerry!"

Immediately the motor-boat commenced to glide down-stream. Frank found that his engine worked like a charm. He could apparently do anything he wanted with it, and the whole apparatus seemed more like a plaything than a powerful motor.

"A good beginning. Hope it keeps up," remarked Bluff.

"Me for a life on the ocean wave," sang Jerry as he coiled the rope ship-shape, and then going forward climbed up on the bow to look out for "snags."

There were numerous abrupt bends to the river just below the Florida town, and with that swift current it was difficult to navigate around these places successfully. By degrees, of course, Frank expected to become more familiar with both the engine and the only way these things could be successfully met. He was always wide-awake, and eager to learn.

Jerry had perched himself on the forward rail, where he could survey the scenery. Will had his camera in his hand, and seemed ready to snap off any remarkable picture that presented itself to his vision. He was keen on taking some views that would embrace the weird, hanging Spanish moss, though Frank told him to have patience, and any number of these would come in time.

There was not the least warning when the shock came. The boat suddenly brought up with a bang on some hidden snag, and as Frank involuntarily shut off the power he had a rapid view of poor Jerry taking a header over the rail. Immediately after, a tremendous splash announced that he had struck the water all right; indeed, as he sprawled with hands and legs outstretched, one would half suspect it was a gigantic frog that leaped from the boat into the deep river.

CHAPTER V

THE FIRST CAMPFIRE

"Tell me about that, will you!" gasped Jerry, as he bobbed above the surface.

He was swimming industriously to keep from being swept down with the current.

Frank, finding that the motor worked smoothly, and no damage had been done by the concussion, started it backing just enough to keep the boat steady.

He darted to the bow, where Bluff and Will were already hanging.

"What was it?" called the swimmer, who, now that he was in, seemed disposed to make a picnic of the affair, after his usual joking way.

"A snag, of course. I thought you were going to sing out if we came on one?" said Frank.

"I did, and you all heard me yell," asserted Jerry.

"Yes, while you were passing through the air. Much good that would do," observed Bluff, disposed to refuse such evidence.

"But there was nothing in sight. The snag must have been

down under the surface, and the water is so brown I couldn't see it. My! but that was a vault! Talk about your high divers, there never was a prettier leap than that."

"Just my luck, again!" whimpered Will. "What a magnificent picture of the Jumping Frog that would have made in our scrap-book. Why on earth didn't you tell me you were going to do it, and I could have been ready to snap you off?"

"Hear that man, with me down in this ooze, soaked to the skin! Wait till I find a chance to get at him!" groaned Jerry, shaking his fist upward, in mock anger, though at the time he was grinning amiably.

"While you are down there, pard, why not take a look, and see if we scraped the paint off the boat's nose when we banged that log," suggested practical Frank.

"That's so. Make the best of a bad bargain. Why, no; nothing doing, boys. This stem is made of solid brass, and could stand many a hard bump. I think Cousin Archie must have been warned in advance, and had her made doubly staunch," sang out Jerry.

"Can you see the snag anywhere around?" asked Frank.

"Not here. Perhaps we're down below it now."

"Or it may have been an alligator, fellows. Some of the natives told me there are a few in this old stream," observed Bluff.

"Yes, and there he is now!" shouted Will. "He crawled up on the bank to dry off, and is going to jump in again! Oh! why *wasn't* I ready! Look out, Jerry! He's coming for you!"

Jerry was already in motion. The notion of meeting an alligator might have appealed to him, but not under these circumstances. He struck out like a madman as he struggled to get to a point where he could reach up and clasp the eager hands extended down to him, for he had heard the splash that announced the reptile's taking to the water.

Of course, the little six-foot 'gator was by long odds the more scared of the two, but then Jerry, being a greenhorn, did not know that. When finally the others managed to drag him, dripping, one deck, he was panting like a tired dog and puffing like a grampus.

"Talk to me about your narrow squeaks, they don't appeal to me one little bit!" he gasped. "Where's the old alligator monster now, Will? Did you snap him off?"

"He never came up again. That's just my luck, you know."

"Better times coming, Will. You'll take many pictures of 'gators on logs and sunny banks before we finish this little trip," laughed Frank.

"Yes, I know what you're laughing at," grunted Jerry, "and I suppose I did look like a big frog as I sailed away off the bow. After this the lookout ought to be tied to his seat. It was lucky, though, you had so little headway on, Frank. We might have ended our cruise half an hour after we began it."

The air was balmy, and Jerry seemed nothing loth to sit there and dry off, as the journey was resumed down the river.

"Any game along here, do you think?" asked Will presently.

"They told me there was plenty, only you have to look sharp, and not get lost in the swamps. Men have gone out hunting and never come back again; though, of course, these were strangers, and not the natives. Nobody ever knew whether they were lost or fell into the hands of some black criminals who were hanging out hereabouts."

Jerry volunteered this information. He was always making inquiries in connection with the possibilities of game.

"I saw a blue heron just then, swinging downstream below us. And there's something snow-white over there. Yes, it must be a crane standing in the water, with his fishing-rod ready for business; and there goes a string of white birds, over yonder. Do you know what they are, Frank?" asked Will.

"I'm not sure, but I think they belong to the ibis family. Look at that 'coon scurrying up that log, running from the water. He's been trying to scoop out a dinner of fish, too. Nearly everything feeds on fish down here, even many of the wild ducks. Got him that time, did you, Will?"

"I think so," replied Will complacently, for he had snapped his camera while the striped "bushy-tail" was still moving up the slanting log.

They were making fair progress all the while. So the afternoon began to wear away. The current was almost enough to carry them on at the rate of several miles an hour. With the prospect of meeting hidden snags at any minute, Frank did not deem it wise to put on any speed. That would come when they were upon the open gulf, and obstacles no longer worried them.

They had entered a section that undoubtedly bordered on a swamp. The trees grew thicker, and shut out much of the light, so that it seemed actually like dusk. And to the delight of Will, the long streamers of Spanish moss hung everywhere.

"Say, perhaps we'd better pull up soon for the night. This sort of work needs all the eyesight we've got, and it's getting some gloomy just now. I wouldn't dare attempt an exposure with this shadow on everything," remarked Will.

"Always something wrong, eh, Will? However, putting the picture-getting aside, you'll admit that this is a mighty comfy position to be in. There's Bluff writing up the menu he expects to spring on us the first meal out," laughed Frank.

"I own up I *was* thinking of something along that line. Wish I had some of the fine oysters they tell us grow down South. Your sister Nellie gave me several recipes to try, and I'm going to spring them on you the first chance, see if I don't."

"Well, I only hope you have better success than the said Nellie usually has. My dad threatens to send her to cooking school before she kills off the entire family with her experiments. But as to the oysters, you must wait till we get out of the river. This is fresh water. Mussels or fresh-water clams grow in such places, but hardly oysters," observed Frank.

"I'm going to tell Nellie what you said, when we get back," declared Bluff.

"Well, it encourages me to know that you expect we will survive the operation. But then, ten to one they are recipes she clipped from some paper, and wants you to try for her. I'm going to keep an eye on you whenever you hang around the fire, remember. You can bear watching," Frank continued.

"Glad to hear that, for some people can't," remarked the other calmly.

At which the laugh was on Frank; but he took it good-naturedly, as always. It required a good deal to make him show signs of being provoked; but like most people of that temperament, if ever he did lose his temper, he was apt to be very angry indeed.

Presently they found what seemed to be a good place to tie up for the night. A small boat, called the dinghy, or dinky, was trailed behind. This might come in handy whenever they wanted to go ashore while the motor-boat was anchored; or one of the boys might wish to use it for fishing, gathering oysters, or shooting shore birds, later on.

The ground being high and dry just at that particular spot, they built a fire and determined to cook supper ashore. There would likely be plenty of opportunities for doing this aboard, later, and they could not resist that chance for an open campfire.

Bluff was assisted by Jerry in getting the first supper. It turned out to be appetizing. They had been in the woods so much now that even the poorest cook in the club, Will, was picking up quite a little knowledge of the art, and felt an occasional desire to show off.

The boys never got over joking poor Will about his first experience in cooking rice, however. He had put the entire four pounds in a pot while the rest were away. One of them, coming back to camp presently, found Will in distress. He had filled every kettle and pannikin with the swelling rice, and despite the glistening heaps the original kettle was still boiling up heaps of it, so that it threatened to even smother the fire.

He knew better now.

After the meal was over they sat around, taking things easy. Frank was writing in his logbook, Will monkeying with his camera, while Jerry and Bluff sat there discussing something that had to do with their respective lung power - a question never, as yet, fully settled, although they had had many a friendly contest to thresh out this rivalry.

"Frank, don't look up, please! Listen to me!" said Will in a low voice.

"Well, what is it?" asked the other, simply pausing in the act of writing a word.

"I saw something moving over behind that bunch of saw-palmettos on your left. Pretending not to be looking, I squinted out of the tail of my eye. What do you think I saw? The head of a black man raised - an awfully wicked-looking head, too, Frank. What had we better do about it?" went on Will, his whispering voice quivering.

"Nothing. Leave it to me. Don't show any signs of excitement, please, but just keep on with what you are doing," and Frank allowed his left hand to slowly creep in the direction where his shotgun lay on the ground.

CHAPTER VI

THE SWAMP FUGITIVE

"Now, my friend behind the bunch of saw-palmetto, won't you join us?"

Frank had slowly risen, picking up his gun as he gained his feet. There was a movement in the quarter where his gaze seemed directed, then a human figure began to crawl into the camp, looking more like a great dog than a man.

"Great Caesar's ghost!" ejaculated Bluff.

"Tell me about that, will you!" exclaimed Jerry, making a dive for his own gun.

"Quiet, fellows! There's no need of any excitement. It's only a visitor from the swamp, come to have a cup of coffee with us," remarked Frank steadily.

He made no attempt to aim his weapon, being satisfied to let the negro see that he was armed, and ready for action. The wretched outcast was almost in tatters. He looked thin and haggard, in marked contrast with the sleek and well-fed darkies the boys had generally noticed since reaching the Sunny South.

Having reached a spot in front of Frank, the man arose to his full height. There was a look of trouble on his face. He had been hunted like a wolf for so long that naturally he believed every man's hand was against him.

But Frank saw at once that Will had been mistaken when he remarked upon the vicious look of the fugitive. He had taken the expression of fear for that of maliciousness.

"Well, who are you, and what do you want here?" Frank asked directly.

The black started, and looked at him a little eagerly.

"I's got lost in de swamp, boss, 'deedy I has, an' I smelled de vittals a-cookin', so's I couldn't keep away. Didn't mean to skeer yuh, suah I didn't. Yuh wouldn't hurt a pore ole brack man, would yuh, little marse?" he droned, still keeping his eyes fastened apprehensively on Frank and his gun.

"I guess it's a fairy story he's putting up, Frank. They told me about him up at the town. He answers the description of George Walden, all right," said Bluff.

Frank saw the man start at mention of the name, and shiver.

"That's your name, all right, I can see. Now, George, what have you been doing to make you hide out like this in the swamp?" demanded the other sternly.

"Reckons as how I ain't wanted 'round dis section, boss. Ain't done nothin' so very ba-ad, but seems like we-uns kain't git on. Some o' the white gentlemen dey got it in fo' me, an' it was either a case o' hidin' out er takin' a coat o' tar an' feathers. I reckoned I'd rather lay in de swamp a while. But, boss, I 'clar tuh Moses I'se mighty nigh starved tuh death, I is."

The man had evidently come to the conclusion that these Northern lads, with the motor-boat, could hardly be hunting fugitive blacks in the swamp. He was beginning to recover a little of his courage.

"How about that, Bluff? What did the people in the town say he had done?" asked Frank.

"Oh, nothing much, only, just as he says, he's an undesirable citizen around the place. I think they said he had a weakness for chickens, and could not keep from sneaking into a coop if half a chance presented itself," replied the other.

Frank smiled.

"Well, I believe that has never been called more than a weakness with a colored man, in the North. People who keep chickens should see to it that a poor fellow is not tempted beyond his strength. Locks are cheap enough. Then our friend George has not been doing anything particularly villainous?"

"'Deed an' 'deed I ain't, boss. I's only wantin' tuh git outen dis kentry. I's got a darter married, an' livin' at Chattanooga. If I kin on'y git up dar, she'd nigh die wid happiness. An' if I felt a little stronger I'd try an' walk de hull way, so I would, young marse!" exclaimed the other eagerly.

They could see him sniffing the air, after the manner of a hungry dog that scents a bone near by.

"Sit down, George. I'm going to make you a pot of coffee such as you never tasted in all your life," said Will at this juncture.

The negro turned his eyes upon him gratefully. He might be a ne'er-do-well, and a genuine nuisance around the town on the river where he had grown up, but to the generous-hearted lads from the North he was only a poor hungry human being, and fortune had been very good to them.

"And I'll cook him some bacon. I bet it's been a long time since he put a bit between his teeth," declared Bluff, wishing to be in the game.

"Good for you, boys! I think, myself, that this old fellow may have been more sinned against than sinning; though perhaps he's wise in wanting to make a change of base since they're all down on him around here. We ought to show our thanks for the many favors that have been showered on us, and the best way to do it is to help some less fortunate fellow."

"Talk to me about your Good Samaritan! We've got several of 'em right here in this camp, and as I don't want to be left out in the cold, I'm going to make George here a present of that shirt I took such a dislike to. He won't mind the objectionable color, I reckon," spoke up Jerry.

The black man sat there, grinning from ear to ear. He could hardly believe his hearing. These campers, whom he had at first feared were there to drag him back to town, so that he might afford sport for the young hotbloods, had turned out to be the only friends he had known for many a day.

He tried to express his gratitude, but, of course, stumbled so that they told him they were ready to take it all for granted.

When the meal was ready he ate until he could contain no more. Jerry watched him with a queer expression on his face, and for once he realized how near starvation a human being may get at times.

At the same time, George was a bit uneasy. He kept looking around, as though he feared lest others might appear who would not be so kindly disposed toward him. Hence, after he had finished his supper, he showed a disposition to depart, telling them that he had a shack in the swamp.

Frank did not attempt to hinder him, for he saw that the man could not wholly get over his suspicion that there might be some trick back of this generous hospitality. George had evidently been educated in the belief that no one ever assisted a black man unless he had an ax to grind.

Before he went they gave him some bacon and a little can of

ground coffee. As Cousin Archie had supplied much more than they could ever use on the trip, all of them thought they could easily afford to be a bit generous, since the occasion had come to their very door, as it were.

When George had faded away in the shadows the boys resumed the tasks his coming had interrupted. Naturally enough, their conversation was in connection with the great questions which the South had had to struggle with since the emancipation proclamation had freed so many million blacks and placed them on their own responsibility.

"I don't suppose any of you want to get the single tent out and sleep ashore to-night?" said Frank finally, as he saw his comrades yawning, as if ready to turn in.

"Not me," answered Bluff immediately.

"Some time later on I'm going to try it, but I want to get used to these queer scenes first," remarked Will.

"He thinks an alligator might crawl up out of the river and gobble him up," laughed Jerry.

"Well, we haven't heard from you yet. Are you getting out the tent?" asked Frank.

"I would, only it's such a bother. On the whole, I'm contented with the snug little bunky on board," came the answer, at which Will shrugged his shoulders, as if to say he knew it would be so.

"All right, then; let's go aboard. I'll fix up the fire here so it will burn a few hours anyway. Kind of cheerful to see it as a fellow sits out his watch. This log, pushed over to the blaze, might answer," observed Frank, suiting the action to his words.

"Then we do keep a watch?" queried Bluff.

Frank looked around at their gloomy and impressive surroundings and then raised his eyebrows in an expressive manner.

"You just bet we do!" exclaimed Jerry. "Here's a swamp with all manner of wild animals in it, from alligators and wildcats to mosquitoes by the million. How do we know but what some of them might take a notion to come aboard in the night? I can see myself waking up to find a bobtailed cat cuddling up under my blanket with me; or a ten-foot 'gator sprawled out across Will, here, asking to have his picture taken. Tell me about that, will you, fellows?"

"And then there may be other coons in hiding here; chaps who are wanted for something far more desperate than poor old George. They might murder us all in our sleep. Oh, yes, let us have a watch, by all means. I agree to sit it out for the first two hours if Frank will take the second," cried Will.

So it was settled. They went aboard, and made preparations for sleep. Of course, there were no regular bunks aboard the *Jessamine*, since the space was too limited to admit of such luxuries. When the cruisers wanted to retire, two of them made beds of the seats, and the others found a suitable couch in the bottom. In case of rain, the automobile top would protect them; but in dry weather it could be left partly off, so as to insure more air.

Frank and Will had the seats first on this night, for it had been so arranged that they would change around each night, so as to give every fellow a chance. As Bluff put it, "just like we were playing a scrub game of ball, each one getting a chance to pitch and catch in turn."

Will took up his place on the side toward the shore. It was some little time before his comrades all settled down, but finally he knew they slept. He sat there, watching the fire burn near by, and thinking of many interesting things, until, on striking a match, and examining his watch, he found that it was time he awoke Frank.

He took the place of his chum when the other assumed the duties of guard, and being really sleepy by this time, quickly dropped off.

Frank sat there, with his gun across his knees, also watching the fire. He had little idea that there would anything occur to disturb the serenity of the night, but believed "an ounce of prevention better than a pound of cure."

"The old log seems to do its duty handsomely, after all. I wouldn't be surprised if it was still burning at daylight," he mused, as he continued to watch the fire creeping along the dry wood and slowly eating its way toward the other end.

Then Frank started, as he saw a distinct movement in a little shadowy spot. It happened that the firelight did not reach this particular place, so that, strive as he might, he could not see distinctly.

"There's something crawling along right there. I can see a dark figure move," he said to himself as he strained his eyesight the harder.

Of course, his first thought was of the negro whom they had just fed. Perhaps to an irresponsible fellow like poor old George the temptation to try and steal something had been irresistible, and he was now creeping toward the motor-boat with the intention of getting aboard and laying hands on anything of value.

Then, again, it might be another entirely, some rascal much more to be feared than George. Frank was not more than half a minute in making up his mind what the best course for him to pursue under the circumstances would be.

"I'll give him a shot, firing far over his head. Whoever it is, the report must make him skedaddle like hot cakes," he thought, for he could not bear the idea of doing a fellow human being any bodily harm, no matter whether he were white or black.

Having so decided, Frank raised his gun a trifle further, so that it bore on the tops of the cabbage palms beyond. Then his finger pressed the trigger, and with the sudden report he gave a tremendous yell.

CHAPTER VII

A FLORIDA SHERIFF

There was an upheaval of various blankets, three faces peeped forth, and then came a wild scramble for weapons.

"Wow! What is it, Frank!" bellowed Bluff.

"My camera! Who took it away from where I placed it?"

"Talk to me about that, will you! That fellow will howl after his blooming box when he goes to cross the Styx after he dies," grunted Jerry.

Frank had paid no attention to his comrades. His eyes were glued upon the shadowy spot where he felt positive he had seen some creeping figure drawing closer to the boat, inch by inch.

They heard him laugh aloud, as though something he had seen amused him.

"Was it a thief? And did you shoot him?" asked Will, appalled.

"A thief, all right; but I didn't shoot the beggar. Wish I had, now," responded the watch, with regret in his voice.

"Then it couldn't have been a human thief, for you'd never say that. Did you see the critter go?" came from Jerry, as he peered forth, gun in hand.

"I fired high on purpose, for I was afraid it might be poor old George sneaking back to see if he could get away with any more of that fine bacon. Whatever it was, it made a flying leap back into the shadows. I thought I heard an angry or startled snarl, but you fellows made so much confusion as you bounced up that I couldn't be sure."

"Jumped away, eh? Then I take it the thing must have been a bobcat," said Jerry.

"Something along the cat family, anyway," replied Frank.

"Look here! You don't mean to say it was - a panther?" demanded the other.

"I'm not saying anything; but in the morning we'll go and take a look at the ground behind that second log over there. If there are any tracks, they ought to tell the story," remarked Frank, who, no matter how positive he might feel that this was just what he had seen, would not commit himself without some proof.

"That's what I get for waking Frank up so soon. Oh! why didn't I hold out a little while longer? Nothing ever happens when I'm on duty, it seems. I must be a Jonah, that's what!" sighed Will disconsolately.

"Why, what would you have done?" demanded Bluff.

"Shot the intruder, but by snapping the trigger of my little flashlight pistol, and in that way I'd have taken a picture of the beast as it crouched there. I sat here, holding that pistol, and my camera, ready, for two mortal hours, in vain. I'm the most unlucky dog going."

"Well, I notice that, after all, you manage to gather in your share of pictures. The trouble is, you want to corral everything going. Well, me to the bench again for another snooze. Wake me when you get tired of sitting up, Frank. If the critter comes again, let him have a charge," said Jerry.

"I certainly will, if I can make sure that it doesn't happen to be a man," was the reply of Frank.

Apparently, the report of the shotgun had alarmed the beast, for he certainly did not show himself again. Whatever it was, the attractive smell around the vicinity of the campfire must have drawn him out of the neighboring swamp, just as it had Black George, earlier in the night.

Both Jerry and Bluff took their turns, and in this way daylight found them undisturbed. Jerry had left his shotgun at home, and carried a rifle on this trip. He and Bluff had entered into many an argument because this new weapon was a six-shot gun; for Jerry had made all manner of fun over Bluff owning a shotgun built after the same principle, nor could they settle the dispute, Jerry claiming that it was all right in a rifle, as a man hunted big game with that, and his life might be in danger; while with the other weapon he usually only shot birds and inoffensive small animals; while Bluff declared that what was black for the pot was also black for the kettle.

Going ashore, soon after getting up, Frank knelt down alongside the log where he had seen the shadowy figure bound off.

"I say, Jerry!" he presently called out.

"Want me?" asked that worthy, folding up his blanket so that it could hang and get the breeze, whether they moved on or remained where they were.

"Yes. Come here. You'll be interested, I think."

Jerry quickly reached his side.

"What's doing?" he asked, eagerly searching with his eyes the ground near Frank.

"Bend lower, for the sign is rather faint. What d'ye make of that, and that? Is it the paw of a bobcat?" asked the one on his knees, with an expressive smile.

"Great Jehosaphat! No! Then it was a panther, after all!" cried Jerry.

"I think I'm safe in saying yes to that question," replied Frank.

"And now don't you wish you'd shot him?"

"Well, yes, if I had been positive, which I couldn't be, under the circumstances, you see. Perhaps I may be lucky enough to run across one of the breed again when there can be no uncertainty, for I would like very much to say I'd knocked over a panther," was the reply Frank made.

"Say! Shall we cook breakfast again on the shore?" called Will from on board the boat.

"We might as well. There will be plenty of occasions when we'll just have to do it aboard, and this fire seems cheerful like," replied Jerry.

Frank agreeing with him, they carried the necessary utensils ashore, and preparations were begun looking toward the getting of a bounteous meal.

"Wonder how our good friend, Black George, feels this morning? Hello! We're going to have visitors, I see. Look what's coming down the river, boys!"

As Bluff spoke they ceased eating and turned to gaze upstream. A boat was advancing rapidly, with the aid of the current and a pair of stout ashen oars. Several men occupied the craft which was quite roomy.

"Say, they've got some dogs there. Ain't those bloodhounds, Frank?" whispered Will, for the boat was now close by, the men craning their necks to look at the launch.

"I believe they are. Perhaps this is the sheriff on the run for our black friend, George," returned Frank.

"Oh! I hope not. I don't believe the poor chap is as dangerous as all that. I have an idea he's more sinned against than sinning," replied Will, who always looked on the better side of those he met, and hence was an easy mark for sharpers.

The men in the boat came ashore. Our friends then saw that the dogs were of a black-and-tan color, with long ears, and the aspect that distinguishes bloodhounds.

"Mornin', neighbors. Takin' a trip down the river, I see. That's right. Like to see youngsters enjyin' themselves. I'm the sheriff o' this heah county, an' these gentlemen is my deputies. We're a-lookin' fo' a desprit scoundrel thet hes been doin' heaps o' mischief 'round heah. His latest work was tuh rob the house o' a cotton planter named Davis, an' nigh about kill the old man. We want him, an' we're jest 'bout determined not tuh go back without the skunk. Don't s'pose yuh could 'a' set eyes on sech a pizen critter, gents?" said the leader.

He was a tall, lean man, with a hawklike nose and keen blue eyes. He wore a long frock coat, considerably the worse for wear, and this, with his slouch hat, gave him the appearance of a Western marshal, in the eyes of Jerry, at least.

"Who was this scoundrel?" asked Frank uneasily.

"His name is Bob Young, an' he's really the son o' a minister upcountry, but long ago his father cast him off as a scamp. He'll sure swing one o' these days," replied the sheriff, looking keenly at Frank, as though he suspected he might know something that he wanted to hear.

"Then he's a white man?" asked the other quickly, and with evident relief.

"Shore he is, an' the toughest ever. Seen any sign o' him, stranger?"

"Not a thing. We had a coon in camp last night, starving, and we fed him. He was Black George, the man they ran out of town some time back," ventured Frank.

He saw that the dogs were nosing about, and feared lest they should set out on the trail of the poor wretch by mistake.

The sheriff laughed.

"Oh, our time's too valuable to fool away with that black trash. He ain't wuth shootin'. Come on, then, boys. Like tuh sit up with yuh, friends, an' have a snack, but we got to be on the move afore the trail below gits cold. Yuh see, we hed word 'bout Bob, an' we wanter git him this clip, sure. So-long, an' good luck! Thet thar is sure the boss little boat yuh got."

And presently the sheriff and his posse faded from view under the long streamers of hanging Spanish moss that overshadowed the river below.

"I'm just as glad. He gave me the creeps. That eye of his was fierce," said Will.

"Oh, that's because you've got a guilty conscience, I guess," laughed Jerry. "Now to me he was a picture of a strong character that would have made a good showing in our album," and he looked severely at Will.

"Oh! What beastly luck! Why didn't I think of it in time? Another chance gone glimmering! I think you fellows are too mean for anything, not to remind me of these things in time. He would have embellished our album handsomely - and those dogs, too! How picturesque bloodhounds are! I feel sick."

Will jumped up, snatched his camera, and stalked off beyond the edge of the camp, as if to brood alone. Presently they heard him calling:

"Oh, Frank! Won't you come here for a minute? I'm just taking the picture of a big snake, and he's as angry as you please. There's a locust somewhere close by, too, keeping up a tremendous rattling. Please hurry! He won't wait long!"

Frank, followed by Jerry, was off like a shot. His face turned white with sudden apprehension as he ran. Coming upon Will, kneeling there, and watching, he seized him by the shoulders and whirled him back, exclaiming:

"Why, you greenhorn, don't you know that's a diamond-back rattler, coiled up and ready to launch himself at you?"

CHAPTER VIII

WILL DOES IT

"Talk to me about babes in the woods!" gasped jerry.

He was staring at the enormous rattler, that still kept up a buzzing with his rattle, and which sound poor Will had believed was made by a locust.

"Shoot the thing, Jerry! You've been wise enough to fetch your gun!" said Frank.

"That just suits me. Have you got all the snapshots you want, Will?" demanded Jerry, falling on one knee and elevating his rifle.

"There! He's reforming! You see, he did actually think of me, for once. Oh, yes. I snapped him three times. I rather think he didn't like the sound, for he darted his head at me wickedly. I suspected it might be a rattlesnake, though," replied the photographer calmly.

Then came a sharp report.

"Keep back!" called Jerry as the snake's folds suddenly flew out; but its head was almost blown from its body, and there was no more danger to be feared.

"I'll get the rattle, to remind you of your narrow squeak, Will," said Jerry.

"That's kind of you, now; but I rather think you are getting it to remind you of your first shot at game with the new rifle," remarked Will.

The others had by now come up to stare at the enormously thick snake, with more or less of a shudder.

"How about having that skin, to make a belt or something?" suggested Bluff.

"You're welcome to it, if you can take it off and properly dry if; but you're so squeamish about snakes I'd hardly think you'd care for the job," remarked Jerry.

"I'll see. I heard Nellie say she always wanted a belt made out of a skin like that, and perhaps I may try to get it," concluded Bluff.

"Are we going to proceed, or put in a day around here, fellows?" asked Frank.

"I say stay. We may not get another chance at a swamp before we reach the open gulf, and I want to snap a dozen fine views off around here. I mean to take the little dinghy and push into the swamp a bit," ventured Will.

"Say! he's getting real venturesome, ain't he?" laughed Jerry.

"Next thing he'll be getting lost, and we'll have a deuce of a time finding him again. Make him take a compass along, Frank, and that old revolver of yours," growled Bluff.

"Don't you worry about me, now. Perhaps you'll find I'm able to look out for myself far better than any of you give me credit for," returned the other, with a show of indignation.

He went aboard to get ready, taking another roll of films

along, for, as he remarked, there could be no telling what might turn up.

"Try to keep your wits about you, Will, and don't venture too far away. If in doubt, fire the pistol three times, and we'll answer you," said Frank, who was not wholly easy about the exploring trip.

"Got some grub along?" asked Bluff, for that was a very essential part of any undertaking, in his eyes.

"Yes to everything. So-long, fellows! Don't let anybody run away with the motor-boat while I'm gone." And, with a merry laugh, Will dipped his paddle into the water, sending the little dinghy gliding toward the more quiet lagoons of the swamp.

He was soon under the spell of his surroundings. These were so weird that the ardent photographer really forgot everything else. As he paddled along he saw a dozen pictures around him, and when he thought the light fair enough he took a time exposure.

So an hour passed away. In all that time he had seen no evidence of life, save a few alligators, some wary 'coons, a 'possum hanging from a tree by its tail, and some birds, mostly crows or bluejays.

In the water he had noted a variety of snakes. Remembering what Frank had told him about these gliding reptiles, Will was careful not to bother with them; for in all probability they were water moccasins, whose bite, if not so deadly as that of the diamond-back rattler, would cause a wound that might never heal, since it seems to put a certain poison into the flesh that brings about a running sore.

Perhaps he ought to go back. He had succeeded in taking all of half a dozen good views, besides several of which he was not so certain.

Then it dawned upon Will that, after all, he was not so sure that he knew which way he ought to go. True, he had a compass, and could tell where the north lay, as well as all other cardinal points, but the question was, did the camp lie east or south of where he happened to be just then?

He cudgeled his brains to try to remember, so as to place himself.

"Say! Perhaps I am lost, all right," he remarked, with a laugh, for it did not look at all serious just then, but more like a joke.

Then he suddenly remembered that he had the only boat.

"If they wanted to hunt for me they couldn't do it. To move about in this swamp without a boat would be impossible; that is, for a stranger; and the launch could never come here. Guess I'll shoot up a few and get my points."

So saying, he banged away three times.

Presently there was an answering series of shots, but very far distant.

"Whew! I didn't dream I'd gone so far," he said, and having noted the direction from which the sounds seemed to come, he started to paddle hard.

After half an hour's work he halted, tired, and perspiring freely.

"This is no fun, I tell you. Wonder if I'm anywhere near? I might try again."

This time there was no answer. The wind possibly kept those in camp from hearing the fusilade. Will began to grow alarmed. It was now high noon, and he felt hungry, so he disposed of the lunch he had carried, at Bluff's suggestion. Incidentally, he blessed his chum for thinking of such a thing.

After that he paddled some more, until he grew very tired.

"This begins to look some serious. What if I have to spend a night here? Gee! I won't like that much, I guess. Hello! What's that over yonder? Seems to me it might be some sort of a shack, made of palmetto leaves. Wonder who lives there? Ugh! What if it turns out to be that desperado the sheriff is hunting - Bob?"

The idea oppressed him, and he felt like paddling away; but his case was desperate, and he determined to creep up and try to ascertain just who lived in the primitive-looking native shack.

So, finding a chance to land on the little island among the dark waters of the lagoon, he started to advance cautiously in the direction of the dwelling, which was really the first Will had seen made of leaves.

In spite of his fears, the fever of picture-taking was so strong in his breast that he had to stop once and level his camera at the picturesque shack. Then the familiar click announced that he had secured what he wanted.

Perhaps that sound may have reached other ears, and been misconstrued to mean something else. Will might have realized this much could he have seen the dark figure creeping up on him, and lying flat on his stomach most of the time.

As the boy reached the lonely shack he was about to put out his hand in an endeavor to draw aside some of the dry leaves so that he might peep within, when, without warning, a heavy form fell upon him, flattening him out on the sand.

CHAPTER IX

THE MOTOR-BOAT AND THE PROWLERS

The unlucky young photographer gave a shriek. He could only think of that panther Frank had seen on the previous night, and believed that he was now in the power of the ferocious beast.

As he fell forward he managed to twist himself around so that he lay almost on his back. This enabled him to look up into the face of the man who was pinioning him down so fiercely to the earth.

"George!" he exclaimed.

It was the same fugitive black who had visited their camp on the preceding night. He stared hard at the face of the one he was holding down.

"Gorry! Am it you, young marse?" he exclaimed, as he released his savage clutch, and even attempted to help Will up.

"Yes. I'm lost, you see. Tried to do too much. Taking pictures in the swamp, and kind of got a little mixed. But I'm glad to meet you again, George. Is this the place where you hold out?"

The negro was breathing hard. He had evidently been greatly excited, under the belief that the creeping form had been one of his enemies, bent on effecting his capture, with the idea of furnishing sport for the idlers at the river town, through the medium of a little "tar and feathers party," so popular in some sections of the Southern backwoods.

"I heerd a sound like it wor a gun bein' cocked. Dat must 'a' been de black box heah, suh. Gorry! but I's glad it wan't dem white trash from de town. I's jest a-gittin' ready tuh vamoose outen heah right smart now. I's gwine tuh Chattanooga, tuh jine my darter. An' dat grub yuh guv me'll kerry me part o' the way."

"That's all right, George. Suppose you just take the time to paddle me back to our camp. I'll promise you a lot more provisions, and some money in the bargain. This is a serious scrape for me, and while my life may not amount to much, it does seem a pity to waste all the fine views I've taken in this old swamp. Will you go?"

"'Deed an' I will, right peart, suh. You-all hev bin mighty good tuh me, an' I ain't gwine tuh forgit dat you sed as how I mightn't be just as bad as dey paint me. Git into de leetle boat, young mars, an' I'll paddle yuh home," said the old negro, with alacrity.

"Hold on a minute, George! I want to shoot you first," observed Will.

"Gorry! Will it hurt, marse?" asked the other, beginning to look worried as he saw the mysterious black box being aimed at him.

"Not one-tenth as bad as having a tooth pulled out," laughed Will. "In fact, you probably would never know it. Please step back a little. You see, I'm trying to get the shack in, too. That's part of the game."

Will snapped the camera shutter.

"That's all. Didn't feel it, did you, George?"

"Not so's I kin notice, suh. An' will dat show me an' de leetle shack w'en it's done fixed?" asked the fugitive wonderingly, eyeing the camera with respect.

"Fine. And if you leave me your address, or that of your married daughter up in Chattanooga, I promise to send you a copy later on, George."

"Oh! I'll do dat, marse, 'deed I will! Nebber hed my pictur' took yet. My gal, she'll be sure surprised tuh see dat!" exclaimed the negro, still grinning.

"Well, we had better go now. Are you sure you can paddle me around to where the boat is tied up, George?"

"Easy as fallin' off'n a log, suh. Git dar in 'bout a hour er so." And George dipped deeply, with the air of one who was accustomed to the paddle.

Indeed, Will learned presently that he had a dugout canoe hidden near by, and in which he was accustomed to navigate the intricate channels of the great swamp. He had lived out here some time, and knew the place thoroughly.

Will was sensible enough not to mention the fact that the sheriff and his posse, together with the two bloodhounds, had passed along that morning. Had he done so, the negro might have taken the alarm, and declined to accompany him farther.

Things had turned out well, after all. If he had a faculty for tumbling into a scrape, at least he was usually fortunate enough to get out again all right.

Before the hour was really up they came out of the swamp, and in sight of the tied-up motorboat. At sight of the dinghy the three boys gave shouts of delight.

"Tell me about that, will you!" said Jerry, as he stared at Will, seated comfortably in the bow of the short little craft, while the old negro, crouching in a limited area farther aft, plied the spruce paddle. "He comes back in style, with a guide to show him the way!"

"Better that than to stay in that gloomy place, eh, Frank? Oh, I got lost, all right, but happened to find the shack of our good friend George, who rescued me."

"Ain't he the honest chap, though? Ready to acknowledge the corn, no matter what the consequences," declared Bluff.

"And I promised George some more of our extra provisions, if you have no objections, fellows. He's going to start for Chattanooga right off. I didn't mention about the sheriff and his posse, for I was afraid it might alarm the poor fellow. Better not say anything to him about it," remarked Will aside.

"And they don't want him, anyhow. Give George just what you and Frank think we can spare. I feel sorry for the old man, too. Say! did you get his photo this time, Will?" asked Jerry.

"Thank you, I did, and standing beside that wonderful shack, made of palmetto leaves. I'm glad to see that you're beginning to take an interest in my work. Keep it up, Jerry. We'll all enjoy the pictures later on," remarked Will.

The boys had eaten lunch, but that did not deter them from getting another ready, and both Will and the negro did full justice to it.

"Here, George, is the package of food for you to carry on your long trip. And I want you to take this, also. It's only five dollars, but it may help out on the way to Chattanooga," said Will, slipping the bill into the old fellow's black hand.

George looked at it as though he could not believe his eyes.

"Five dollahs! Gorry! dat am mo' dan I done see dis t'ree yeahs, suh! Five dollahs! If I kin on'y keep dat till I sees my gal,

Cleopatrick, how her eyes'll stick out!" he said, scratching his white wool in delight, while his eyes glistened.

"Say that name again, will you?" murmured Jerry, gripping the arm of Frank as if taken suddenly ill.

"Cleopatrick. Dat's my darter, suh. She married a right smart nigger, an' he's got a barber shop up dar. His name it am Samuel Parker White, an' if so be yuh ebber wants tuh send me one ob dat pictur', jest drap it dar. I's over-whelmed wid gratefulness, 'deed I is. Dey won't ebber be troubled wif George Duval 'round these diggin's ag'in, dat's so, suh."

"But think of the henroosts up there about poor old Chattanooga," said Jerry in Frank's ear, though the latter frowned at him for saying it.

After a short time old George took his departure on foot. He said that it was his intention to start immediately for the North. He had a few things at his shack he wanted to get, when he would depart from the soil of Florida forever.

"Happy Florida!" muttered the irrepressible Jerry.

Nevertheless, each of them shook the old darky's hand, in parting, and wished him the best of good luck.

"Well, what had we better do, boys?" asked Frank when they found themselves once more alone.

"I'm for getting out," said Will.

"That surprises me some, for it was you who wanted to stay," remarked Bluff.

"Well, we stayed, didn't we? I only want to mention the fact that I'm satisfied, if the rest of you are. I've secured all the swamp scenes I care for," retorted Will.

"I say move on. We can find a better place than this to sleep to-night. Why, the skeeters nearly carried me away last night," declared Jerry.

"And I'm beginning to be anxious, myself, for a glimpse of that wonderful gulf, not to say a taste of those delicious oysters," put in Bluff.

"That settles it, then. Let's get the things aboard, and drop downstream a few miles, anyway."

Frank suited his action to his words by picking up some of the cooking utensils and starting to clean them. This task was soon accomplished, and by degrees all their property that had been taken ashore was stowed away on the boat.

Then finally, Jerry, whose business it seemed to be to mind the hawsers, unfastened the rope that held the bow of the boat, still pointing with
the current, just as they had stopped.

"Tell me when!" he called out as he stood by to repeat this maneuver with the second hawser at the stern.

The motor began to chug away cheerily.

"There's life about that sound, all right," laughed Will, who had been impressed with the dreadful monotony and stillness of the swamp.

"Let her loose!" called Frank, at the wheel.

So they once more started toward the open sea. There were still quite a few miles to be traversed, however, before they could set eyes on that same open water. The river was as "crooked as a New York alderman's record," as Jerry declared, and so it was that in order to advance five miles in a straight line they were compelled to navigate three times that distance on the water.

When the afternoon had waned they found a good place for a halt.

Again they cooked a royal supper. When four healthy boys are off on a lark of this sort the subject of eating is always one of their chief concerns, which must account for the space which it occupies in records of cruising and camping trips.

Will did not go ashore that evening. Indeed, somehow, none of them cared to stay alone, though Jerry did build up quite a roaring fire, just because he was fond of seeing the flames leap up in frolic.

As before, they divided the night into four watches, and this time Will chose to take the one that would bring him on deck from about midnight to two.

When it came his turn he sat there holding his camera faithfully, and hoping for something to happen; but it did not come, and he was finally forced to arouse Bluff to take his place.

The latter did so rather unwillingly. Bluff was unusually sleepy, it seemed, and inclined to believe that this watch business was all humbug, anyway. What did they need to fear? Possibly there was not a human being within five miles of where the motor-boat was tied up.

So Bluff grew a bit careless. Two or three times he napped while on duty, and as nothing came of it he made up his mind that there could not be any danger. So he settled himself more comfortably on the seat and allowed his eyes to close once more.

How long he slept Bluff never knew. He was awakened by some sound, but he could not tell what it was.

He did not move, but sat there trying to remember just where he was, and after satisfying his mind with regard to that point, wondered what it was that had disturbed his dreams.

Not hearing any repetition of the noise, he was about to drop off again, his eyes feeling very heavy, when he saw something move. Was that Frank, or one of the other boys, who had been ashore, climbing back to the boat?

Bluff gripped his gun, and kept on the watch. Whoever it might be, he evidently did not want to arouse the sleepers, for he was very careful how he stepped after he had come aboard.

Bluff caught a glimpse of the other's face as the dying fire on shore chanced to flare up. He made the alarming discovery that it was a white man, but a stranger; and then and there he remembered about the sheriff's hunt for the desperado!

CHAPTER X

BLUFF'S FIRST 'GATOR

"Don't you move a hand or foot, you rascal!" cried Bluff sternly as he suddenly sat up, with leveled gun.

The unknown pillager was only a comparatively few feet away, so that it was easy for him to see the weapon covered him. Immediately he elevated his hands, as if to signify that he surrendered.

"What is it, Bluff?" asked a quiet voice, and Frank appeared from the bottom of the boat.

By then the thief must have determined that unless he took chances he would be made a prisoner. He gave a sudden yell, and threw himself over the gunwale of the boat. By chance it was the side toward the water, and they heard the splash that announced his arrival below.

"Some fellow aboard, bent on stealing everything we had!" exclaimed Bluff.

"Was it George?" gasped Will, aghast at the possibility of such ingratitude.

"No; a white man. See! There he goes, swimming across the river!"

The light was not very good, but they could see a sort of phosphorescent glow on the water, where some object was struggling for the opposite bank.

Bluff half leveled his gun, when Frank shoved it aside.

"You wouldn't want to kill him, even if he is a desperate case. I guess he got little or nothing. Let him go. The sheriff will be along after him soon," he said.

"But what is that trailing after him, Frank?" echoed Will.

"Where?" demanded the other quickly.

"Why, look right there! And whatever it is, it's catching up with him fast, too! I believe it must be an alligator!" exclaimed Will.

"I had a glimpse of a big fellow hovering under the boat at dusk. I think he was after the refuse we threw over. Would he hurt a swimmer?" asked Bluff.

"I don't know. I wouldn't want to try his appetite, that's all. Could you give the beast a shot without hitting the man, Bluff?" asked Frank eagerly.

"Why, yes; for at this short distance the shot won't scatter much."

As he spoke Bluff took quick aim. He was only too glad to be able to make use of his gun in so good a cause. The thief might be all they painted him, and yet he was a white man, and a minister's son in the bargain, the sheriff had said.

With the heavy report there was a combination of sounds. The man in the water gave a yell, as though he fancied the shot had been aimed at him. A short distance away, the water was being threshed wildly by some unwieldy object.

"I hit him all right!" shouted the excited marksman.

Some vigorous language came floating across from where the man was now dragging himself out of the river.

"Say, Bob Young! You didn't think we shot at you, did you? There was a big 'gator after you, and he'd got you, too, only for that shot. Better make yourself scarce around these regions. The sheriff is after you, with dogs and a posse."

Frank called this out after the fleeing shadowy figure that was just halting on the edge of the bank opposite.

"Thanks!" came in a hoarse voice, followed by a reckless laugh. "But he'll find it a hard job to corner me, you bet!"

That was the last they ever saw of Bob Young. In the morning, sure enough, the baying of a hound was heard, and presently along came the sheriff with his two dogs and the grim deputies.

"Mornin', boys! Reckon yuh may 'a' seen sumpin o' my man this heah time, as he's sure been close tuh yuh!" he called out while still some distance off.

"Yes. He tried to rob us last night, and jumped overboard when discovered," returned Frank.

"And swam across to the other side. He was followed by a 'gator, that might have got him, too, only for our chum, Bluff, here, giving the reptile a shot," proceeded Jerry; while aside he said: "Get busy, Will, with that shebang of yours. Now's your chance to snap him off!"

"What's that, suh? If anybody tries to snap me off they're sure liable tuh get punctured some!" exclaimed the sheriff, whose ears were as keen as his eyes.

Frank laughed as he said:

"He means with a camera, Mr. Sheriff. My friend was sorry he didn't get your picture before, that's all. But if you want to cross over we can let you use our little dinghy here."

"Now, that's very considerate o' yuh, suh. I accept with pleasure, and when we round that rapscallion up, as we surely will before callin' the game off, yuh can have the satisfaction of knowing yuh hev helped the forces of law an' order, suh, to put an end tuh the career o' a most notorious rascal. I neglected tuh tell yuh before that this Bob Young is wanted fo' many crimes."

Frank tied a long rope to the dinghy, so that after the sheriff and his men and dogs were well over he could pull the boat back again. The dogs swam across, and the three men filled the small craft so full that there was danger of its capsizing.

However, they managed to get over in safety, and Will took a fine view of the strange ferry, with the dogs swimming alongside, while they were in midstream. The sheriff was so obliging as to actually pose for the picture.

"Heah's yuh 'gator over on the bank, suh. He must have crawled out to die, a most unusual thing for the varmints to do, as they generally sink like a rock, tuh stay down fo' several days!" he called out.

Then the posse vanished on the fresh trail of the desperado.

"I rather think they'll get Bob," ventured Frank. "That sheriff is a determined man, and he's enlisted in this hunt for keeps. How about going over to view the remains, Bluff?" he asked as he pulled the dinghy in.

"That's just what I was about to propose. My first 'gator, so perhaps I'd like to get his hide, if possible, or some of his teeth, anyway," returned the other, getting into the small boat with Frank.

Sure enough, they found a dead alligator up on the bank. The load of shot, fired at such a short distance, must have gone pretty much like a bullet. Some of them had entered his protuberant eyes, and by accident must have pierced his brain.

"A lucky shot, all right. I don't believe it could ever happen again, especially when the one who fired was almost behind the 'gator," commented Frank.

"How big is he?" asked the one who had slain the reptile.

"I should say all of ten feet, perhaps even eleven. They seldom grow bigger than twelve down here, I'm told, so this one is something of a whopper. If the alligator man I talked with at Coney Island a year ago told the truth, then this one must be several hundred years old."

"Whew! Perhaps he saw Columbus land!" suggested Bluff humorously, for he could not quite believe any such tale.

He concluded merely to knock out a tooth or two, to remember the event, but when Will heard about it he insisted on being ferried over so as to get a picture of their first Florida 'gator, with the proud Bluff standing beside it, to prove its length.

They got under way about eight o'clock.

Just at that time Jerry said he heard some distant shooting. It seemed to come from the direction the sheriff and his party had gone, so they wondered if they could have come up with the fugitive Bob, and whether those shots had any reference to the two hounds.

"I think the fellow must have been armed, and unless his gun became useless after his bath last night, his first care would be to shoot down the dogs, so as to cut off pursuit," ventured Frank.

They afterward learned, however, by making inquiries, that the sheriff got his man, wounded, and that Bob later on paid the penalty of his crime.

By noon that day they came to a sawmill, where a party of convicts, under guard, were making cypress shingles. Our boys did not put in, for the sight was anything but pleasing to them; although Will did think it wise to get a picture of the camp, so as to add variety to his collection.

About three o'clock they suddenly came to a little town. Here they stopped only a brief time, Frank going ashore to post some letters and purchase a few things he had on his list.

Once more they were afloat.

"I've got some pleasant news for you, fellows," said Frank, about an hour or so after they had lost sight of the settlement in the woods.

"Along what line?" asked Will.

"I think I can guess. For some time I've been sniffing the air, and ready to declare that it had a whiff of salt in it!" exclaimed Jerry.

"And I could, in imagination, smell those fine fat oysters roasting," said Bluff, smacking his lips in anticipation.

"You're on, all right. The gulf is close at hand. Indeed, I'm adding a little speed just now, in the hope that we may be able to open it up before night," remarked Frank.

"How about that bend, just below? Somehow, it strikes me that once we round that something may be doing. It's just a sneaking notion, but you wait," ventured Jerry.

Ten minutes later they swept around the bend in question, and a cry burst from every lip, for there, in the light of the declining sun, lay the great Mexican Gulf, stretching as far in the distance as the eye could see.

The river cruise was ended, and another kind of adventure lay before them.

CHAPTER XI

ALL THE COMFORTS OF SALT WATER

"Why are you slowing up, Frank?"

"Yes, just when we ought to make a grand burst of speed, too," said Jerry.

"You forget that the sun is low, and evening close at hand," replied Frank,

"Tell me about that, and what it has to do with us. I'm a greeny when it comes to running a motor-boat."

"Oh, the boat has little to do with it; but please remember that the Gulf of Mexico is a larger affair than Camalot Lake. In fact, it means the ocean, with all that implies. Suppose we were caught off-shore the very first night with no place to go?"

"That would be tough, for a fact. I think I see what you mean, Frank. We'll anchor in the mouth of the river to-night - is that it?" continued Jerry.

"Just what I wanted to say. Then in the morning, after we have studied our gulf chart, we can lay out our day's work, if the wind is favorable."

"Wind! Why, we can go whether it blows or not!" ejaculated Will, who had already taken a snapshot of the picture presented by the open water beyond the island in the mouth of the river.

"Particularly when not. If anything of a south wind is on, the waves are apt to stagger such a little boat as this."

Frank had kept his eyes about him while he talked. He now brought the *Jessamine* alongside the bank at the most favorable spot he could see.

Jerry was ashore immediately.

"Make her additionally secure to-night," said Frank.

"Why, what d'ye expect - a hurricane?" And Will looked anxiously at the clear sky.

"Oh, I guess not; but you see we are now in the region of tides, and a change might swing us around, perhaps break the boat away from shore. We'd feel nice if we woke up in the morning to find ourselves out of sight of land," laughed Frank.

Of course he was joking, but Will looked serious for some time. He even went ashore, after Jerry had finished his job, and Frank, watching out of the corner of his eye, was amused to see him bending down and examining the ropes, as if to make certain they were securely tied.

Will was the possessor of a different nature from his three chums. He could show courage, when necessary, but, as a usual thing, was much more given to sentiment, and in physique he could hardly compare with any of the others.

Bluff had also gone ashore, and vanished from view. Frank could easily give a guess as to what sort of an errand he was on. It hardly needed glimpses of him bending over the spots where there were shoals along the tideway to understand that he was looking to see whether the one dearest wish of his heart was about to be fulfilled.

"I guess he'll find some, at last," laughed Frank, after calling Jerry's attention to the fact that the other had gone.

"Bluff is daft on the subject of oysters, all right. He never seems to tire of eating them in season, and yet he says he never picked one up on the spot where it grew. He seems to be coming back, Frank!" exclaimed Jerry, who was working with some fishing tackle that he had found aboard, and which Cousin Archie had used before in Southern waters.

"Hey! They're right here, and in tremendous quantities! Where's that oyster knife, Frank? Give it to me, please. I want to try a few right on the bed where they grew. Give me a tin kettle, too, and I'll open a mess for supper!" cried the boy ashore, as he reached the boat.

"Take care you don't cut your fingers. If these oysters are small, and stand up on edge, in clusters, they're called coon oysters, and have a sharp shell that is like a razor," said Frank as he handed the articles over.

"Why coon oysters?" demanded Bluff, who always wanted to know.

"Perhaps because they lie on shore, exposed at low water, and the 'coons manage to get a mess occasionally," put in the wise Jerry.

So Bluff hurried away around the bend, to amuse himself to his heart's content opening native oysters right where they grew, something he had looked forward to doing with almost childish delight.

Jerry, having arranged his tackle, got ready to do a little fishing, for it was still half an hour to sunset. He had discovered that there were mullet jumping out of the water here and there, "acrobats of the gulf," Frank called them.

Among other things aboard the motor-boat they had found a

contraption which Frank said was a small Spanish cast-net. It had a row of leads along the bottom, with leading strings passing up through a central ring. Frank had read directions how to use this, and he amused himself making a few trials while Jerry was busy.

At first he came near pulling a few teeth out, for it is a part of the program that one of the leads must be held between the teeth while others are gathered up in the hands as the net is flung out over the water by a sharp rotary motion that spreads it open as it strikes.

The leads instantly sink, covering a space often ten feet or more in diameter; then, by drawing quickly at the rope, the cords are pulled through the ring and the net closes in like a purse, holding whatever fish it may have covered when thrown.

After a few trials Frank succeeded in catching a couple of silver mullet that had been unable to escape his clumsy attempts.

"I'll get the hang of it after a while," he said, as he tossed these into the little dinghy where Jerry was taking his place, "but those may do you for bait this evening, old fellow."

"Bully for you, Frank! Always coming to the rescue. I was just wondering what I should use, and had an eye on some big blue crabs swimming along there on the bottom. With the dip-net I might have caught a few. If Bluff sees them he'll never stop talking about fried crabs." And Jerry pushed off.

"Good luck to you, sportsman!" called Frank.

He had a number of things he wanted to do himself, and only cast an occasional glance out to where Jerry had anchored the dinghy, opposite to where the motor-boat was tied up.

Will was fussing around, doing something or other. He always made so much bustle whenever he had anything on hand that his chums frequently called him an "old woman," but this never seemed to bother the ardent photographer, who pursued his way in spite of laughter or ridicule.

After a while he came and sat down near where Frank was arranging the three little single blue-flame stoves that formed the cooking range of the boat.

"I was just thinking, Frank," said he, "that I've never heard you say a word about that mysterious packet your father entrusted to you before we left home."

"Well, I've often thought about it as I felt it in my pocket, but you see there's nothing to be done until we sight Cedar Keys. Then I'll break the seal and read further directions," replied Frank.

"Of course you've speculated about it?" went on Will.

"Lots of times, but always arrived at the same old point - that I couldn't guess in a year what it meant," laughed the other.

"Do you think it could be a joke?" asked Will.

"Never. My dad was too serious when he gave it to me; and besides, he never jokes like that. We must wait a little while, and then learn the truth. Depend on it, he had a good reason for what he did. I expect we'll get something of a big surprise."

"There comes Bluff, and I really believe the fellow's got some oysters opened, by the way he carries that kettle," said Will.

"And just look at the expression on his face, will you? A fellow who had won a first prize in school could hardly seem more tickled."

"Oh, I've got 'em, all right, boys, about a big quart, too, and only cut myself half a dozen times," cried Bluff, laughing as he scrambled aboard.

"And I give you fair warning that those cuts will hurt worse to-morrow than they do now. Let me see. Well, they do look pretty fine. I reckon you've got lots of broken shells in with the oysters, so I'll take care to strain the mess. How shall we have them for the first, boys?" asked Frank.

"I'm just hankering for scalloped oysters, but perhaps a stew would be easier to start with. We have the unsweetened milk, you know, and they say that answers first rate. How are you on that, Frank?"

"I can manage it first rate. Are you fond of a stew, Will?"

"Yes. I like them any way. But I was watching Jerry out there. What under the sun is he doing?"

Frank cast a quick glance out over the water.

"He's got a fish on, and it seems to be a big one, too!" he exclaimed.

"Why, it's pulling his boat around like fun! Look at that, will you? Say! be careful, Jerry, or overboard you go!" shrieked Will.

"There! He's headed this way, now, and going faster than ever! I never saw such a thing before, in all my life! What can it be, Frank?" cried Bluff, excited.

"I don't know for certain, but I'd venture to say he's fast to a shark!" answered Frank, hurrying to the side of the motor-boat to see better.

"A shark! Great Caesar's ghost! What will become of him? Why, the brute is carrying our pard off! There he goes, faster and faster, and headed straight out toward the open gulf! Jerry, let him go!" called Will in his excitement.

Jerry, in the little cockleshell of a dinghy, was whirling past as this cry rang out. He turned to wave a hand at his chums, and they heard him singing:

"A life on the ocean wave for me, my boys!"

CHAPTER XII

THE BREAKDOWN OF THE MOTOR

"Say! he's going off, dead sure!" exclaimed Will, in distress.

"He certainly seems to be having a free ride out to sea," remarked Frank.

"But that little craft will upset, and let him drown, Frank! Can't you stop him from such mad capers?" continued the other.

Frank put his hands up to his mouth in such fashion that they formed a sort of megaphone, and allowed his voice to carry far.

"I say, Jerry!" he bawled.

"Hello!" came faintly from the onrushing fisherman, who was sitting in such fashion as to properly balance his small pumpkin-seed-shaped craft as it sped over the water, so rapidly as to leave a sheet of white foam behind.

"Cut loose! Danger!" shouted Frank.

"Did he hear you, Frank?" asked Will anxiously.

"I guess so. Anyhow, he seems to be moving toward the bow, where his line is fast. I hope he has a knife with him, that's all," replied Frank, straining his eyes to see what was going on, for the sun had set, and already dusk was just commencing to gather over the water.

"He always carries one in his fishing bag," declared Bluff, not a little alarmed himself over this new source of danger, so utterly foreign to anything they had ever experienced before.

"There! He's done it! Hurrah!" shouted Will in relief.

"I bet he hated to let that thing go!" said Bluff, who knew the determined nature of the fisherman full well.

"And he's lost his line, and the hook, too," commented Will.

"That's of little consequence, for there are plenty more where they came from. I'm glad he was sensible enough not to carry the joke too far," observed Frank.

Jerry came paddling slowly back. Apparently he wanted to continue his fishing, but his good sense told him the hour was really too late.

"Talk to me about your toboggan slides! What could compare with that jolly old dash? Peary wasn't in it with me. I've heard of boats pulled by dolphins, but give me a shark every time for a racer. I'm only sorry I had to cut loose so soon," he said as he came aboard.

"I see you have one mullet left, Jerry. After supper we'll get out a couple of lines, and fish from the motor-boat. Perhaps we can pick up a channel bass or a weakfish, which I am told they call a sea trout down here."

"A good idea, Frank. I'll just get the lines ready while you look after supper. Glad to see Bluff managed to find his oysters. Perhaps we'll have a rest now, and he'll quit sighing after the same. But they look fine and dandy, too."

The boys did not wonder so much now at the size of the hooks they had found in Cousin Archie's assortment of war material, each of them fastened on a heavy but pliable brass snell, and with copper wire instead of thread. Florida sea fishing requires such heavy tackle, because one is never certain whether he may hook a forty-pound channel bass or a shark, and an ordinary hook would be quickly torn loose.

The oyster stew turned out well. Every one was loud in praise of its splendid qualities, and Bluff was given to understand that they did not care how often he supplied the larder with a pail of fresh bivalves.

He did not seem just quite so eager to promise, and Frank suspected that those nasty little cuts on his fingers were beginning to be painful.

The supper over, the boys sat around, taking it easy, and looking out upon the open space where they knew the mysterious gulf lay, about which they had read so much in the past.

Once they saw lights moving along, which must certainly have belonged to some sort of craft, either a steamer bound for New Orleans, or else some private steam yacht, the owner of which was cruising in these sub-tropical waters for pleasure.

Jerry had cast out a line from the bow and a second one from the stern. As the depth of water was good, it did not much matter how far from shore the bait lay.

"Hope something gets hold before we turn in," he said, after carrying out his part of the program.

"Yes; fresh fish for breakfast wouldn't taste bad," remarked Bluff.

"Bah! That's the only thing you think of, Bluff. Now, if you had any genuine sporting blood in your veins it would be the last thing you bothered about. Let me shoot the game, or catch the fish, and I don't care who eats them," said Jerry.

"All the same, I noticed that you passed up your dish for a second helping of stew," remarked the other instantly.

"Pure philanthropy, my dear boy, that's why I did that," answered Jerry.

"Huh! How do you make that out?" demanded Bluff.

"Why, you see, I was afraid you'd make yourself sick eating so much, and out of the goodness of my heart I sacrificed my better feelings in order to save you."

Bluff said nothing, but the grunt he gave was deeply significant of skepticism.

While they were talking, a while later, Jerry suddenly gave utterance to a whoop, and sprang to where one of the lines was fastened. This he began dragging in, although it seemed to take considerable effort.

"He's a dandy, all right! Frank, get Cousin Archie's gaff hook, and stand ready to yank him aboard when I get him alongside!" he called.

This was finally accomplished, and with considerable splashing a magnificent bronze-backed channel bass, weighing at least twenty pounds, was captured.

The boys were delighted. Here was a new treat, indeed. In comparison with the trout and black bass that had, up to now, constituted their only game fish, this was tremendous. Still, later on, Frank was satisfied that a one-pound black bass, held with a light fly-rod, could give more sport to the square inch than any fish in Florida waters.

There was nothing more doing up to the time they went to bed. In the morning they found the hook gone from the other line. Frank said they must have caught a shark, or else another large bass, which, in twisting about, had broken the tackle. Still, they were not sorry, for they would not have known what to do with more.

"That's what I call fresh fish," said Bluff, as he sighed because he could not eat another bite of the tempting dish.

"It does go pretty good," admitted Jerry, with a wink toward Frank.

Sometimes Frank was of the opinion that the name of "Bluff" had been bestowed on the wrong fellow, for Jerry was inclined to play the part much more than the one who bore the odium that went with the name.

"Now to get under way and move out on the gulf!" exclaimed Will, in some excitement, as the breakfast things were put away and the deck cleared for action.

Frank had taken a careful observation, and announced that there did not seem to be any reason why they should linger there longer. His chart showed him a refuge some fifteen miles along the coast, to the east, where they could run in should it be deemed necessary. If the weather kept good they could speed another fifteen miles, and make a second lagoon sheltered behind outlying islands.

These things are easy enough to plan. It sometimes happens, however, that in attempting to carry them out a hitch occurs which no one has dreamed possible. Now, it might come in the shape of sudden winds that kick up a tremendous sea; again, there might be a breakdown of the motor, as may happen with any boat, no matter how well built.

They made a flying start, and all the boys were thrilled when they found themselves far out from land, and headed along the coast, toward the east. Later on, of course, their line of travel would be south, as the coast turned and they drew nearer to their destination, Cedar Keys.

Everything seemed to be working nicely, and they had soon put half a dozen miles behind them. Frank was attending to the motor, while the others lay about on the deck, watching the heavens or the surrounding water.

Not a breath of wind seemed to be blowing, and the sun came down with summer heat, causing coats to be discarded by all hands.

"Hey! What's that? Where's the blooming shore gone?" suddenly exclaimed Bluff.

Frank raised his head at the cry.

"It's a fog coming up!" he said uneasily, for that was the one thing he had dreaded most of all while out upon the open waters of the big gulf, and no haven near at hand.

With incredible swiftness the blanket seemed to sweep over the surface of the sea. In ten minutes they were completely surrounded, and could not discern any object fifty feet away.

"This is awkward, fellows; but perhaps it may not last long. Meanwhile, we will have to steer by the compass. All of you listen to hear the wash of the rollers on the beach, if we happen to get in too close," said Frank, trying to keep calm.

They continued along for half an hour, under reduced speed. Still the fog remained as dense as ever. Frank was wondering if they might not pass the first haven without knowing it. He thought it was very unfortunate that such a thing as this should occur on their very first day out.

"Hello! What are you stopping for?" demanded Jerry suddenly, as the sound of the bustling little motor ceased and the boat slowed down.

Captain Quincy Allen

Frank was bending low over the machinery.

"I don't know, fellows, but something has happened to the motor. That stop was none of my doing; but I hope it won't amount to much," he said cheerfully.

The other three looked at each other uneasily. With the motor broken down, and surrounded by a treacherous fog, out there on the big gulf, their situation was one well calculated to cause alarm.

CHAPTER XIII

LOST IN THE FOG

"What's to be done?" asked Will presently.

"I'm looking the motor over, first of all. Perhaps it's a small matter, and I can fix it up. Sometimes these new machines act a bit cranky. Want of oil will even bring about trouble. Jerry, you take a look with me. Two heads are often better than one," said Frank.

"Can we do anything?" questioned Bluff.

"Just try and see if you can hear a sound like water washing up on the beach. We couldn't land with this boat as though it were smaller."

"That's a fact. Say! if we were in our canoes, now, how easy it would be to run up on that same beach, lift the jolly little craft out, and go ashore! As it is, we must stay afloat, and take the chances of a storm coming up."

"Storm!" echoed Will, looking hastily around. "Oh, come, now! You don't think there can be any danger of that happening, do you, Frank?"

"Hardly. If a little breeze rises, it may carry this beastly old fog away, and then we can see where we are. Meanwhile, Jerry and I will try to find out what it is that makes our motor balk just when we want it most."

They sat there for a long while, Bluff and Will looking this way and that, to see if there was any object near by; but only that heavy blanket of sea fog surrounded them.

"Do you hear the roll of the water on the shore still?" asked Frank finally.

"I haven't for some time, now," admitted Bluff.

"And I was just wondering, as I sat here and watched the water as it flowed past, whether we were not drifting out further all the time," suggested Will.

"Say! what makes you think that? Seems to me you're always scaring up ghosts, and making things look blacker than they are," grumbled Bluff.

"Well, you just watch that water passing. What does that mean, eh? Something is moving all the while, and it's either the boat or the tide," claimed Will.

Frank stuck his head over the side and gave a look.

"He's right about it," was his speedy comment. "The tide is carrying us out all the time, and that's why you don't hear the sound of the rollers on the sand!"

"Wow! You're giving it to us good and hard now. That sounds like trouble. This old gulf is some wide, I know, and it'll take us quite a spell to cross the duck pond at this rate!" exclaimed Bluff in dismay.

"Can't either of you find out what's wrong with the engine?" asked Will.

"We think we've guessed it, and we're working on that line now; but it may take some little time, so don't get impatient," returned Frank.

If he felt any alarm himself, his manner did not indicate it; but then Frank had a faculty for disguising his feelings when it would add to the comfort of his chums.

So the old state of affairs continued, he and Jerry with their heads bent low over the machinery, and the others sitting there on deck, exchanging doleful words from time to time, and surveying that gray blanket that wrapped them in.

"How far do you think we've gone from shore?" asked Will finally.

"I was just trying to figure out from the way that water runs past. It's going faster than we are, you see. I should say we might have drifted several miles since the motor broke down," replied Bluff soberly.

"I wonder how deep it is here?"

"Say! what do you talk that way for? Think we'll have to swim for it?" exclaimed Bluff, in new alarm.

"Oh! I hope not. You see, I was thinking that if we could reach bottom it might be worth while to anchor here. That would save us from getting any further from the shore, at any rate," replied the other.

"Frank! Listen to what Will says!" called Bluff eagerly.

"What is that?" And Frank's head came into view.

"He says we might try and see how deep it is here; that perhaps the anchor rope is long enough to reach bottom, and we'd stop drifting out to sea."

"Good for Will! That's a bright idea, now. Suppose you two fellows try and see if it will work? Jerry and I seem to be getting on, and there's hope that we'll have things moving presently."

Accordingly, Bluff took up the anchor, which lay forward, and gently dropped it into the smooth water. Then he allowed the rope to pass slowly through his hands.

"Why, it's on bottom already! I don't believe it's ten feet deep away out here, Frank!" he said hurriedly.

"Yes, I've always read that it was shallow along this coast. That makes it more dangerous for vessels of any draught, for they're apt to go aground. Fasten the cable to that cleat, Bluff. Make it secure, for we don't want to lose the whole outfit overboard," remarked Frank.

"That feels a whole heap better," remarked Bluff, settling down again.

"Yes, for we're not moving out further all the time, anyway. Hang this old fog! Why did it want to come up on our very first day, and before we had become used to our strange surroundings?"

"Well, we've got to just take things as we meet 'em, as Frank does. You notice that he seldom finds fault with the way things happen; just puts his shoulder to the wheel and lifts it out of the rut," remarked Bluff.

"Yes, I know that; but every fellow doesn't happen to be built just the same way. I wish I could take things as cool as he does; but I never even snap off a picture without feeling more or less excitement quivering my nerves."

"I don't suppose, now, you could get a decent picture of this?" Bluff suggested.

"What! The fog? Bless your innocent heart, no! What do you think it would be like - just a dreary blank plate. You can't see anything, so how could it show up in a picture?" jeered Will.

"I wonder some bright genius hasn't discovered some sort of magic glasses that will let a fellow see through fog? What a blessing they would be to sailors, and the pilots of ferryboats in New York harbor," observed Bluff thoughtfully.

"Suppose you devote your spare time to solving that riddle? Listen! Was that a shout then?"

"Sounded like it to me; but who would be shouting out here in the fog?" replied Bluff scornfully.

"Come, now. We may not be the only pebbles on the beach. Perhaps there are others marooned out here in the fog, and they may be shouting just to keep their courage up, or for some other purpose," replied Will stoutly.

"Well, the fog won't last much longer, anyway, and that's a comfort."

"How do you know that?" asked Frank, looking up.

"Because I just felt a puff of air. The wind's going to rise, and that means an end to the fog," replied Bluff confidently.

"Well, I only hope we get this motor fixed before it rises too much," and once more Frank gave his full attention to his work on the obstinate engine.

Bluff and Will looked uneasily at each other.

"What does he mean?" asked the latter.

"I think he means that if the wind came up strong the sea would rise, and we couldn't hold out here with our anchor," replied Bluff.

"In which case?"

"We'd either be blown out to sea, and be in danger of foundering, or else driven toward the shore, perhaps to stick half a mile off and be wrecked."

"I don't like either of those propositions any too well. Oh! I hope they get the motor working! I'm so nervous I feel like shouting; and it seems to me I can hear something moving all the time," went on Will.

"Something moving?" echoed his companion, looking at him as if he wondered whether the other could be going out of his mind.

"Yes, over there to windward, which, I take it, is about due west just now. Hark! Didn't you hear that? - and close at hand, too! What can it be?"

"I don't know. Something is moving through the water! I can hear a gurgle and a creaking noise. Do you think it could be a boat bearing down on us? Oh! what if they ran us down in this fog? I say, Frank!" called Bluff, also excited by this time.

"Well, what now?" demanded the other, again appearing in view.

"There's something doing over here. Will thinks it may be a boat coming down on us, full tilt, and liable to grind us to powder."

Frank listened for just three seconds. Then he made a dive for a locker, as if he thought the situation more or less desperate.

"What's he after?" exclaimed Will, amazed.

"That blooming conch-shell horn of Cousin Archie's. He's going to let those chaps know there's another boat out here, and that they don't own the earth, that's what."

And that was just what Frank meant to do. Seizing the conch-shell, from which the point had been cut, he blew a piercing blast that could have been heard a mile off. Again and again he sent out the warning sound, and presently an answering blast came through the dense fog, now swirling madly with the increasing breeze.

"They're right on us! There! I can just make out the top of a mast! Frank, they will run us down!" shouted Will, while the other continued to blow his horn with renewed vim, and the advancing gulf sponger came plunging straight toward the anchored *Jessamine*! It was a thrilling moment for the four chums.

CHAPTER XIV

A CRY ACROSS THE LAGOON

"Keep off, there!" shouted Bluff.

"Luff her, you!" howled Jerry.

"Too-oo-t! too-oo-t!"

Will was the only one of the quartet unable to give utterance to his feelings. He could only cower there, and gape, while the unknown sailing craft was bearing down straight for the little motor-boat, and apparently bound to smash her in two.

Those on the sharpie may have been extremely reckless in thus spreading their canvas to the favoring wind before the fog had lifted enough to allow a decent lookout, but they had some thought for their own safety, however little they cared for that of others.

Hearing the clamor dead ahead, the fellow at the tiller managed to suddenly shift the course of the advancing boat, and just in time. They swept past the *Jessamine* with hardly a yard to spare.

The staring and shivering boys caught a glimpse of several rough men on board the passing sharpie, and what they thought was a girl's head thrust out of the cabin.

Some loud and vigorous language was carried back to the ears of the chums as the fleeing sharpie vanished once more in the fog wreaths.

"Talk to me about that!" exclaimed Jerry indignantly. "They nearly run us down through their own carelessness, and then revile us for getting in the way!"

"Some people never believe there can be two sides to any question. They are always in the right," commented Frank.

He showed little signs of any excitement; yet, did his chums but know it, there was much of thanksgiving in his heart over the narrow escape.

Once again he and Jerry set to work at the stubborn motor, while the others endeavored to keep a sharp lookout. Will, in particular, was holding his head cocked on one side, as though eager to catch the first faint sound of any advancing vessel from windward.

From time to time Bluff amused himself in making dreadful noises with the conch-shell horn, for one has to learn how to sound this before being able to send a ringing blast that can be heard an almost incredible distance.

"Anyhow, the fog's getting thinner all the while," remarked Will joyfully.

"That's a fact," said Frank, glancing up from his work.

A minute later there was a whirr.

"Hurrah! She works!" shouted Jerry.

"Thank goodness! Then we're saved!" echoed Will.

"Get up your anchor, Bluff," remarked Frank quietly.

This Bluff did with cheerful alacrity, and immediately the little motor-boat began to churn the water with her accustomed zeal.

"How long had we been sitting there?" asked Jerry.

"Just two hours," was Frank's reply as he consulted his little nickel watch.

"And now what?" demanded Will.

"We'll move in toward the shore somewhat, and wait for the fog to sweep away. When that happens perhaps we can get our bearings, and find out whether we've passed our first intended refuge or not," returned Frank.

"But you think we have?" queried Bluff.

"Yes; and consequently, as we don't want to turn around and go back, we might as well head for the second harbor."

"What sort of a place is that?" asked Bluff, always seeking information.

"As near as I can make out from the chart, it is a lagoon formed by a long island that stands as a shelter between the open gulf and the shore. There are many such along the gulf coast, and small vessels are in the habit of running behind them when the weather outside gets stormy."

"Hear! hear! Frank's already showing signs of becoming a real old salt. Look there, fellows! Oh! it's gone, now!" cried Jerry, pointing.

"I had just a glimpse of it. That was land, all right, Jerry; and perhaps we'd better alter our course a bit now, heading due east so as to skirt along about this distance out."

So saying, Frank gave the wheel a little whirl, and the

motor-boat, in response, curved gracefully a few points to the starboard.

"Don't she run like a duck?" said Bluff enthusiastically.

"There's the land again, boys! No question but what the fog is being driven off by the wind," remarked Frank.

They could see the shore from time to time, and every one realized that the enshrouding curtain was fast vanishing.

"But, my! isn't it getting rough?" exclaimed Will.

His remark caused the others to look at the speaker.

Frank needed only one glance to tell him the story. Will was already beginning to feel the dreadful nausea of seasickness. The boys were accustomed to spending much time on the water, in their canoes, but little Lake Camalot, at home, and the big Mexican Gulf, were two entirely separate affairs. Indeed, there was only one among them who did not experience at least a trifling indisposition before this first day's voyaging on the salt water was done, and that was Frank himself.

When the fog had entirely vanished the scene was quite picturesque, with the shore and its palmetto trees standing out beyond the heaving billows; but, alack and alas! the artist of the expedition, for once in his life, seemed not to care a picayune whether he ever took another snapshot again or not.

Even Bluff's raillery failed to enthuse him, and the look he cast toward the shore was most pitiful and woebegone.

Seeing this, Frank took pity on his sick chum.

"Hand me that camera, Bluff; and you, Jerry, grab hold of this wheel here. Keep her just as we are, and dodge the big waves as they come, or else we'll all get a beautiful ducking."

Saying this, Frank waited until a good chance came, and then snapped off a couple of views of the turbulent scene.

"Thank you, Frank, for I couldn't have stood up to do it, for a kingdom. I reckon I'll never forget this experience, and every time I see those pictures I'll have a qualm. Oh! I feel so sick, fellows!" wailed Will.

They laid him, groaning, on a blanket, under the protecting hood. No one cared to stay with him more than a minute, for, truth to tell, neither Jerry nor Bluff were in a condition to say how long it might be before they would be feeling just as badly as their chum. Fresh air was invaluable under such circumstances.

Frank, as they boomed along in this boisterous manner, was watching the shore. He expected at any time, now, to discover signs of the refuge which he had mentioned to the others, though it would require sharp eyesight to distinguish the island from the background of shore line.

"What time is it, Frank?" asked Bluff finally.

"Oh, about three, I should say. Time has slipped away, you know."

"What! And nobody ever thought of eating a bite about noon?" exclaimed Jerry.

"Eating!"

Bluff uttered only the one word, but his horrified expression struck Frank as being so comical that he roared with laughter.

"I give you my word, fellows, that this is the very first time since I've known Bluff that the idea of a meal seemed repulsive to him," he declared.

"Please don't, fellows!" came from Will, under the shelter; and in sympathy for him the subject was dropped then and there.

Jerry interested himself in keeping watch with Frank. Between them they managed to decide just where the expected island held forth. The course was altered enough to bring them closer, yet at the same time avoid falling in the trough of the great waves, that might have capsized the motor-boat, once they got a fair sweep at her, broadside on.

"It's the island, all right!" exclaimed Bluff presently, as they drew nearer.

"And we will have to take some chances in getting back of the shelter. You see how the wind blows, and the waves run. Now, please don't bother me. It will require some close calculating to just scrape in without a disaster."

Frank set himself to the task. Mentally, he hoped most fervently that the motor would not take a notion to act contrary just when so much depended on its stability and faithfulness.

Gradually the island began to stand out more distinctly, on their right.

"We're making it, I do believe!" yelled Bluff.

"Why, sure; and the water is getting less rocky already," declared Jerry.

"There you go, copying Frank's salty ways. But I'm not going to dispute it now. I'm only too glad of the chance of resting on smooth water again, whether it happens to be dusty or rocky," avowed Bluff, looking cheerful again.

Even poor Will managed to drag himself out from his shelter to take a dismal, though eager, look. He had the appearance of one who had passed through a long siege of illness, such is the rapidity with which this dreadful malady downs its victims.

"There's one boat already anchored behind the island further on," remarked Jerry.

"I was looking at that fellow," remarked Frank, "and unless I'm mistaken, that's the identical sharpie which came so close to running us down in the fog a little while back."

"You don't say!" exclaimed Will, beginning to grow interested.

It is wonderful how quickly one recovers from an attack of this sort when smoother water is reached. Will was commencing to lose a little of his ghastly whiteness already, while Bluff had started to sigh, as though he thought of supper.

After they had found a safe asylum behind the island Frank thought it best to anchor. He did not care to go too near that sharpie, for the recollection of the three rough spongers or fishermen on board deterred him from wanting to renew their acquaintance.

Bluff immediately bailed out the little dinghy, and set himself to the task of hunting along the shore for oysters. They saw him dipping his arm down again and again, which would indicate that his quest was proving successful. Even Jerry declared that he was now becoming fairly ravenous, and could enjoy a solid meal.

"It's going to be a gloomy old night, fellows. Clouds gathering there in the southwest. From what I've read about the signs, we may have one of those northers boom down on us before morning," remarked Frank.

They were sitting around, enjoying the supper, as he made this remark. Evening was close at hand. The sun had set in what seemed to be an angry glow, with yellow predominating.

"Are we safe right here, if the wind chops around, and comes out of the north?" asked cautious Will.

"Yes, for that arm of the land will shield us all right," declared Jerry.

So the night set in. Darkness gathered unusually early, it seemed to the chums. They had made all arrangements looking to the raising of the complete automobile cover of the boat in case of a downpour.

"I guess there's nothing to fear from the elements," remarked Frank finally.

"Can there be from any other source?" demanded Will, quick to take the alarm from the tone of Frank's voice.

"I bet Frank's thinking of those three blooming pirates who wanted to smash us out on the big water," declared Bluff quickly.

"I confess they were in my mind; but, so far, they've paid no attention to us, and we're a quarter of a mile away from that sharpie. Don't bother your head about them, Will. Of course, we'll keep a watch, as usual, though."

"You just make up your mind we will, now. I didn't like the looks of the crowd a little bit. Some of these wild waterdogs along the gulf coast, they told me, wouldn't object to a little piratical business on the sly when - "

Jerry stopped short. Over the water, from the direction of the mysterious anchored sharpie, had come a strange cry, that seemed to be in the voice of either a woman or a child. The four chums sat there and stared at each other in consternation, for it seemed as though that pitiful cry was for help!

CHAPTER XV

A VISIT TO THE MYSTERIOUS SHARPIE

Jerry made a reach for his gun, that happened to be hanging from a couple of hooks close by his hand.

"Oh! What was that?" asked Will in a trembling voice.

"Sounded to me like a child. I reckon they've got a boy along with 'em, and the brutes are whaling him!" growled Bluff.

"It's a shame, then, that's what!" declared Will, showing unwonted anger, for, as a usual thing, he seldom gave way to his emotions in this line.

They listened for a time in silence. Jerry declared that he felt sure he heard a sound not unlike a child crying, but the heavy voices of the men drowned this.

"Can't we do anything?" asked Will.

"Well, we're only a lot of boys, and they are big strapping men. Probably they've got the law on their side, too," suggested Frank, shaking his head.

"What do you mean by that, Frank?" queried Bluff indignantly.

"Why, the chances are ten to one that the boy, if it is a boy, must belong to one of the men - his own son, I mean - and you know, Mr. Lawyer, that a fellow has to be mighty careful how he steps in between a man and his son. That same law allows even a brute a certain right to punish a rebellious child," said Frank.

So they talked it over a long time. Apparently, nothing could be done that night to ascertain the cause of the outbreak. All was silent now in the direction of the sharpie, and not even a riding light marked the spot where the boat lay.

Frank had recommended that they put out their own lights, all but one lantern, which was to be fastened in such a way that it would mark the anchorage of the little modern motor-boat.

"It'll be an invitation to the sharks to visit us," remarked Bluff.

"Not at all. If they mean to drop in on us during the night, the presence of one lantern, or its absence, will make mighty little difference," responded Frank.

"Do you really think they'll do anything?" asked Will pointedly.

"No, I don't. In the first place, they must know that there's quite a crowd of us aboard. Then such boats as this are apt to carry a few guns along. Just sleep in peace, Will. The chances are ten to one the only thing apt to arouse us to-night may be the howl of a norther," said Frank soothingly.

About ten o'clock both Bluff and Will began yawning.

"Go to bed, you fellows. Jerry and I will manage the first and second watches between us. If we want help, we'll knock you up," observed Frank.

He gave Jerry a wink at the same time, as if to notify him to remain up; and the observant Jerry understood that Frank had a card of some sort up his sleeve.

"Say, what's in the wind?" he asked in a whisper, when they were left alone.

Frank put his finger on his lips, as he said in an equally guarded tone:

"Not so loud. I don't want them to hear."

"Then you really expect trouble with those rascally spongers?" demanded his chum.

"That depends. But I'll tell you what I've decided to do, Jerry."

"Go on; I'm all ears."

"After a bit, I'm going to take the dinghy and paddle over to that sharpie. Somehow or other, I feel that there is some one there in need of assistance. Perhaps it's none of our business, and I'm silly to even think of running such a risk, but something seems to impel me to go; I can't tell you just what."

"Not alone, Frank? Why not take me along, too?" pleaded Jerry.

"No. One can get along in that stumpy little boat fine, while with two it is a clumsy affair. You know that. I only mean to hover near, in the darkness, and find out, if possible, what's doing. Perhaps I may not go closer than fifty feet - unless something happens!"

Jerry did not insist. He realized that what Frank said was the truth, for he had had experience with that same cranky little craft when a second party occupied a place in it.

They sat and talked in low tones for half an hour. Frank made all his plans, and arranged with his chum a set of signals by means of which they might communicate with each other even while both were unseen.

"It's getting darker all the while, I do believe. Sure you know where to find that sharpie?" remarked Jerry as he saw his comrade beginning to make a move.

"I located her by some palmetto trees that stand up high above all others on the key there. Unless they've changed their anchorage, which is unlikely, as we would have heard the noise, I can go straight to the spot," replied Frank confidently.

"Taking your gun along, of course?"

"I think it wise. Those are tough fellows, and there's no telling what might happen. Better be on the safe side," remarked the other sagely.

"Well, I'm going to keep my rifle close by, I tell you. And Bluff has his Gatling gun on the hooks, where he can get hold of it in a hurry. But I hope we don't have any need of them," continued Jerry as he assisted Frank to climb over into the little dinghy astern, where the light of the lantern did not penetrate.

"Be careful how you shoot, at any time, and listen for my signal. I'd hate to be peppered with shot, or get a bullet in my shoulder from my chums."

"Oh, you can depend on me to keep a sharp lookout; and no danger of any accident like that. I never act on impulse, like Bluff. Good-by, and good luck, Frank!"

The dinghy dropped astern with the flowing tide, and was immediately swallowed up in the gloom, which, as Jerry truly said, seemed more dense than ever as the clouds gathered overhead and shut out even the light of the stars.

Frank took up the paddle and set to work. He was by this time something of an adept in the use of a spruce blade, as most canoeists become in time. That is, he could propel a boat silently, not a swirl or a dripping blade betraying the labor that sent it on. Guides in the Maine woods had taught Frank how to approach a deer at night time on a lake without hardly rippling the water.

In this wise he approached the spot where he knew he would find the mysterious sharpie anchored.

Presently he could see the tops of its tall masts against the dark sky; but only for the fact that he was looking for this, it would have passed unnoticed.

There was not a light about the boat. Listening, Frank could hear no sound at first, but as he drew silently nearer he fancied he caught what seemed to be an occasional deep sigh. Then, as his eyes sought the outlines of the little gulf vessel he detected what seemed to be a bowed figure at the stern.

It was from this point that the sighs seemed to come, and he fancied that the huddled-up object must be the figure of a boy, placed on watch while the three big hulking men slept in the cabin near by.

Now he caught the sound of heavy breathing, bordering on snores. From the fact that these suggestive noises were partly muffled, he believed they came from inside the sharpie's cabin.

Foot by foot Frank found himself nearing the stern of the sharpie. He did not need to use the paddle at all, for the current was gently wafting him along in just the direction he wished to go.

So softly did he come that when he reached the sharpie's counter all he had to do was to just put out his hand and fend off.

He now saw that it was really and truly a boy sitting there. The other seemed to be not over ten years of age, judging from his size. He was barefooted, and without either hat or coat, though the night was getting cold now.

Several times he sighed deeply, and once Frank was sure he heard what seemed to be a stifled sob, as though he would have cried had he dared.

Obeying an impulse he could not control, Frank put his hand on the other's arm, at the same time whispering softly:

"Don't make a noise, please. I'm from the other boat, and I want to help you, if I can. You may trust me, my boy, to the limit!"

The crouching figure started, and Frank saw a small face bent down close to his own; then a trembling hand caught his, and there came a whisper:

"Oh! if you only could get me out of this scrape! I'll die if I stay here! They kick me and beat me terribly! Please take me away, mister!"

Frank's first impulse was to draw the lad into the dinghy, then his natural caution caused him to hesitate.

"Who are you, boy?" he whispered.

"Joe Abercrombie; and I guess it's near killed my mother, because they think I run away," came the quick answer.

"Is your father aboard this boat?"

"I ain't got any father. He's dead long time ago. I live with my mother and sister down at Cedar Keys. Please get me off here, mister! I'll do anything for you, if you only can!" the boy kept on saying, and unconsciously raising his voice in his excitement.

Frank's determination was taken. He would accept the chances of trouble and assist this poor little chap, whose condition seemed so miserable, as the slave of the trio of big, rough spongers.

Before he could say another word, or draw the boy into his dinghy, a gruff voice came booming out of the cabin:

"Hey! Who yer talkin' to out thar, younker? Wake up, fellers! I reckon we're boarded by some reptiles! Hank! Carlos! Git at 'em!"

"Oh!" exclaimed the lad piteously. "They've heard us! They're coming out to kill you! Don't stop for me, but go!"

But Frank Langdon was not built that way.

CHAPTER XVI

JOE

With one sweep of his arm Frank drew the little fellow into the dinghy.

Then he snatched up his paddle, and dipped it deeply into the flood. The corklike boat answered instantly to the demand, and backed away from the side of the anchored sharpie.

Even though but a few seconds had passed, the racket aboard the boat had become tremendous by now. The men were shouting at each other as they groped around in the dark for the boy.

Frank knew that the very sounds they made were apt to assist him in his escape, for they helped to drown what little noise he was compelled to make in his quick and positive work with the paddle.

Then one of them must have reached the conclusion that the boy had been kidnapped by some unseen visitor, coming in another boat.

"Keep still, you fools, an' listen!" he shouted.

They seemed to guess his reason, for the chorus of loud voices ceased. Frank also stopped paddling, momentarily. He hoped the listening spongers would be unable to locate him in the darkness.

"Have they any small boat?" he whispered in the ear of the cowering boy.

"No. It broke loose three days ago, in a squall," came the reply.

"Bully!"

That one word expressed all the gratitude that was in Frank's heart. It seemed as though fortune was acting mighty kindly toward the rescuing expedition.

Just then there came a flash and a sharp report. One of the men had fired in the direction he believed the passing boat to be lying.

The bullet splashed in the water, and seemed to go humming over the surface of the lagoon. Then a shout came from the sharpie:

"I seen 'em then! Hey! You thar! Come back with that kid, or it'll be the worse for ye! D'ye hear?"

But Frank, instead of wasting his breath in replying, was once more paddling industriously. He had changed his course, in the hope that should a second bullet follow the first, it might not touch either himself or his charge.

Just as he anticipated, there was a second shot, followed by half a dozen more, seemingly fired at random.

No damage resulted, and Frank believed the incident was closed, at least as far as immediate results went. He now headed directly for the motor-boat, the swinging lantern guiding him.

Those on the sharpie could be heard talking loudly, as though endeavoring to get the truth of the affair, and doubtless making terrible threats as to what they would do to the audacious invader later on.

Frank gave the signal agreed on with Jerry, and in another minute he was lifting his charge aboard the anchored boat.

"Don't ask questions now, fellows," he said, realizing that the others were all agog with excitement, and both Bluff and Will consumed with curiosity. "We must douse the glim, and in the dark change our anchorage. Then, if they come poking over here to-night, looking for us, they won't find anybody at home."

"Hear! hear!" muttered Jerry, who in an emergency always looked to Frank to do the right thing.

He immediately extinguished the light.

"Don't make the least noise, if you can help it. Get the anchor off the ground, but don't attempt to bring it aboard," continued Frank in a whisper.

"Going to start the motor?" asked Bluff.

"Certainly not! It's shallow here, and the push-pole will have to move us along." Saying which, Frank possessed himself of the useful article in question, without which no small boat ever cruises in Florida waters.

"I hope we don't get mixed up, and run afoul of those chaps," breathed Will.

"I've got them located, all right. We'll go in closer to the island, that's all. Perhaps they won't come at all until daylight."

"But if they do, Frank?" asked Bluff.

"We've got a right to protect ourselves, and we will," declared the other between his set teeth, for he was now silently pushing with the pole, Jerry having raised the anchor at the bow.

This sort of thing kept up for ten minutes. By that time Frank knew they were as close to the shore as prudence allowed.

"Let the anchor sink slowly, Jerry, and don't make a sound, if you can avoid it," said Frank.

"It's already on the bottom. Why, we're in only four feet of water here!" came back the whispered answer.

"Now what about the boy you pulled off that craft?" asked Bluff.

"Come here, Joe," said Frank kindly.

Instantly he felt a hand clasping his eagerly, and a boyish voice exclaimed softly:

"Oh! I wanter thank you ever so much for what you did, and my mom'll say the same thing when she sees you!"

"That's all right, Joe. All of us are only boys, older than you, of course, but ready to hold out a helping hand to a poor chap in trouble. Suppose you tell us, in a whisper now, what brought you aboard that sharpie. Who are those three men, and how did you happen to be sailing with them?"

"They're Hank, and Carlos, the Cuban, and my Uncle Ben," came the reply.

"Hello! He's got an uncle aboard!" said Jerry uneasily.

"But he's the worst of the whole lot. He beats me, and calls me bad names. My mother is afraid of him. She didn't want to let me go on this trip with Uncle Ben, but he just made me. His name is Baxter. You see, he's her brother-in-law, not her real brother. I always called him uncle, but he ain't, either. I hate him, and I'd sooner die than go back there again!"

"Don't be afraid, my boy. We have no intention of letting them get you again. It happens that we're bound for Cedar Keys ourselves, and we'll see you safely home. Your mother lives there, you say?" went on Frank, patting the trembling little hand, with its hard palm, that told of much hard work for so young a lad.

"Yes, sir; but we're awful poor. We used to live in Pensacola when dad was on his job, but he got killed in his engine long ago. Then mother had a chance to do something in Cedar Keys, and we came on. But things went wrong, sister got sick, and it's been hard work to get enough to eat. Still, my mother never complains; she ain't one of that kind; and a feller just has to be up and doin' somethin' to help out. That was why I came along when Uncle Ben promised good wages, and without letting her know."

It was a whole life story in a nutshell. Frank had never come so closely in touch with tragedy before. He continued to squeeze the hand he held, while deep down in his heart the generous fellow was making resolutions that would bring a little of sunshine to the Abercrombie home when they landed in the key city.

"Well, we'll have lots of time to talk all these things over tomorrow, and the other days to come. The rest of you pile off again, and leave me here to sit out my watch. I promise to awaken you if anything threatens us," he said finally.

A place was easily found for little Joe. Indeed, as Bluff remarked in a whisper, the motorboat seemed capable of expansion.

"Just like an elevator or an electric car, there's always room for just one more," was the way he put it.

Frank sat there, listening and thinking, for a couple of hours at least There was no alarm. Once he thought he heard sounds such as might be made by the movement of a push-pole; but if so, the searching party failed to locate the anchored motor-boat in its new lodgings.

Jerry took his place a little later, and then Bluff wound up the night, Will being allowed to sleep in peace.

Frank was up at peep of dawn. The masts of the sharpie stood up plainly through the dim light, showing that apparently her anchorage had not been changed at all.

Signs of life were to be seen aboard, and smoke arising from the cabin gave evidence that the three rough spongers were getting their frugal breakfast. Doubtless this caused them to vent their anger anew, for it had been a part of the boy's work to cook.

"The anticipated storm petered out, anyway," remarked Jerry at his elbow.

"Which may be a good thing for us. Possibly we might want to get out of here in a hurry, although I'm averse to running away like a frightened duck," remarked Frank.

"I say stick it out, and give them tit for tat. We're armed, and can make a pretty good showing," declared Bluff, also turning up after hearing voices.

So they began preparations for breakfast, Frank keeping an eye on the sharpie meanwhile. He expected that the trio of spongers would not be likely to pull out without some show of threatening the four who comprised the crew of the motor-boat.

Joe proved to be a bright-faced lad, once the grime was removed, under the influence of salt-water soap and a rough towel. All of the outdoor chums were glad that they had found a chance to be of service to one in distress, for Joe insisted that he never could have stood the vile treatment he was receiving, and meant to run away at the very first opportunity.

They were just sitting down to breakfast when Will gave the alarm.

"They're pulling up anchor, fellows, and hoisting sail. From the appearance of things, we'd better look out for squalls," he announced.

Each of the other three quietly reached around and seized a gun. Will, not to be outdone, picked up the instrument with which he did most of his shooting, his beloved camera, and waited for a chance to snap off the ugly faces of the spongers.

CHAPTER XVII

STUCK ON AN OYSTER BAR

"Do you think they'll attack us, Joe?" asked Jerry as the sharpie began to head straight for the anchored motor-boat.

"No, I don't. Them fellers is big cowards, and when they see the guns they'll take it out in talking," came the prompt answer.

"I believe Joe is right. They must be cowards, or they'd never have abused a boy as they did him. He showed me a lot of bruises from kicks he's had," observed Frank, with a gleam in his eye and a look on his face that told of his detestation for the brute who could, in a temper, knock a child down.

"Say! Perhaps it might be just as well to get the anchor up, and start the motor, in case we wanted to move, anyway," remarked Bluff.

"A hunky idea!" echoed Jerry.

Frank himself agreed to it. So while Jerry hastened to get the mudhook aboard, Frank bent down over the motor. They heard him crank it, and then came the merry and suggestive hum that bespoke business.

"Now, if we wanted, we could go spinning away, and laugh at them," observed Will.

"But we don't intend to, all the same," said Frank quietly, making his appearance again, gun in hand. The boat had moved a length or so, and then floated on the smooth water of the lagoon.

A shout from the sharpie had told that the spongers believed they meant to run off, and at the same time one of them was seen flourishing a gun.

"Hold up, there, you rascals, you!" came across the water, and a shot followed, the bullet splashing close to the motor-boat.

"Don't you try that again, there, or we'll give you a broadside! Do you hear?" shouted Frank, as he and his chums lifted their array of weapons so that the men could easily see what they were up against.

The sharpie kept pushing on until close by. Then a sudden shifting of the rudder caused the boat with the tall masts to "come to" in the wind, with her dingy sails shivering as they hung there lifeless.

"We want that kid!" called a tall, gaunt man with a red beard.

"That's Uncle Ben!" exclaimed Joe, who was peeping over the gunwale.

"Well, you'll have to take it out in wanting, then, because you're not going to get him. Joe says you beat him. He prefers to stay with us, and we're going to take him home to his mother in Cedar Keys. Get that?" called Frank.

The three men conferred together for a minute or two.

"Say! my breakfast's getting cold! I wish they'd hurry," remarked Bluff.

Will was getting busy himself. The old familiar click announced that he had secured a picture of the three spongers at a time when they stood out plainly.

"Hey, you fellers! What yuh mean a-comin' an' stealin' my nephew out o' my boat? He signed for the cruise, he did. It's ag'in the law, what yuh did, an' yer liable ter git yerselves in trouble," the red-bearded man now called.

"We can stand it if you can. The marks on this boy will settle your case for you. Better go on about your business. We don't want any fight, but just make up your minds that if you start it we're going to shoot holes through every one of your crowd. That's enough talk. Now, twenty-three for yours!"

It was seldom that Frank used slang, but just then he was in want of a better expression by means of which to give vent to his feelings.

Bluff was already sitting down and eating, though he kept hold of his gun at the same time, like a true soldier on duty. The trio of spongers talked among themselves for a short time, then, with many harsh words, they pushed their boat around with a pole until the dingy canvas took the breeze again, after which they sailed away.

"A good riddance of bad rubbish," declared Bluff, with his mouth full of bacon; and the others voiced his sentiments exactly.

As for the boy, he was smiling as if tickled over the wonderful change that had come about in his fortunes. Frank, remembering the limp form squatting in the stern of the sharpie, so given up to despair and bodily anguish, could hardly believe that this bright-faced lad was the same.

They did not linger long after finishing breakfast.

While the weather remained favorable Frank thought they ought to be making further progress along their way. True, Cedar Keys was not so very far distant, but who could say what difficulties they might encounter from time to time?

"It will do to loiter when we've arrived within a dozen or two miles of the city," he remarked, and they all admitted the wisdom of his decision.

They went out the same way they had come in. Joe said it was safer, since the lagoon was exceedingly shallow at the east end of the island, and they stood to get aground if the tide was falling, as seemed to be the case.

As they came out from behind the key they discovered the sharpie far away to the west, careening over under a brisk morning breeze, and looking like a dun-colored frightened bird.

"We're not apt to see anything of that tough lot again, I guess," quoth Jerry.

"They're heading for a favorite ground. I didn't know they hunted sponges so far north, Joe. Key West seems to be the head center for the business."

"Get a few, but not many. Mostly fishing and turtling. Some look for coral on the bottom. Lots of ways to earn a living around the water in the gulf," replied the boy, in answer to Frank's inquiry.

"I should say there were. A man need never go hungry in this region if he knows enough to let strong drink alone," said Will.

"That's the trouble with Uncle Ben; he's drunk half the time. And when he is he wants to fight everybody. We all tried to keep away from him," observed Joe.

They were now out upon the gulf again. Will was a little dubious, remembering his bitter experience of the preceding day, but to his surprise and delight, he did not seem to feel the least bit sick. Perhaps the motion was entirely different, for they were now running almost directly into the light breeze.

Frank had turned the wheel over to Bluff, and was conning his charts, with Jerry bending over his shoulder.

"There's where we are right now. Looking along the shore, you can see where a key offers the same sort of refuge we enjoyed last night. In cruising along this coast, it's the only thing to do - run behind one of those islands each night. Only big boats anchor off shore. It's too dangerous for little craft, for a storm is liable to spring up during the night."

In this way Frank went on. They decided that since there seemed to be several possible havens ahead, they had better keep right on until the day waned, or they found themselves forced by a change in the weather to seek shelter.

Jerry had a line trailing astern, with a hook at the end, to which he had attached a bit of white rag. In less than ten minutes after he threw it out he pulled in a gamy fish that might have weighed a couple of pounds.

"A cavalli," said Joe; and they were glad indeed to have a native along who could post them on such things as might have puzzled them.

"Good to eat, is it?" asked Jerry, eyeing the forked tail, which, in this fish, resembles that of the Spanish mackerel.

"Fine. Not so good as pompano, but better than bonita," was Joe's verdict.

"All right. He looks good to me," said Bluff. "Do it some more, Jerry. We need a couple more to make good all around."

"Now, talk to me about that, will you! Listen to how the greedy fellow gauges everybody's appetite by his own voracious longings."

But in spite of his talk, Jerry, being a sportsman to his finger-tips, as he was fond of saying, was only too glad to make a second trial.

This time he had hardly half of his line out when there was a sudden vicious jerk.

"Wow! Nearly took a finger off then! Look at the line whizz, will you? Must have struck a whale!" he cried. But, after all, it was another cavalli (sometimes called crevalle), and not much larger than the first.

So the sport went on until he had brought five to the boat, when he gave up.

"Too hard on the fingers, boys. You see, we're spinning along at a lively clip, and a two-pound fish feels like a ton. I'm all in," he explained.

"Well, we want to keep the fish until evening. Will, here, is dying to clean them for us," said Frank.

"No! no! That is my part of the work!" exclaimed Joe, nor would he hear of anything else.

Noon came and went. Their progress was altogether satisfactory. All of them admitted that outside of that one puzzling breakdown, the motor was working like a charm. It was indeed a pleasure to lie around and see the green waves flashing past, with the picturesque shore only a mile or so away.

Finally Frank announced that he had discovered the island for which he was aiming. They had made a splendid day's showing, and logged more than thirty miles, against a head wind and sea.

Frank tried to follow the chart, but he knew he would have more or less difficulty, for back of the key it was exceedingly shallow, and the channel narrow.

Speed was reduced as they started to enter the open bayou. Jerry, up in the bow, was using the pole as a sounding line, and calling out:

"Two feet! One and three-quarters! One and a half! Hey! Hold up, there! We're on an oyster bar, for sure!" And the grating noise that immediately followed told that they had lost the narrow channel again.

CHAPTER XVIII

TROUBLE

"Oysters! Yum! yum! Who said oysters?" cried Bluff, crawling forward to look.

"Just jump overboard, and you'll get your fill - millions of 'em around!" declared Jerry, prodding with his pole in an effort to release the bow of the boat, but in vain.

"Hold on, there! Don't you do it!" cried Frank as Bluff gave indications of being half inclined to betake himself to the water.

"Why not?" asked the hungry oyster fiend plaintively.

"Because you'll cut your shoes to ribbons on the sharp edges, and perhaps your feet, in the bargain. Remember what you got before," said Frank.

So the impatient one refrained, but he cast many envious looks downward, and a little later could have been seen stretched out on his stomach, prying off bunches of the 'coon oysters with a knife, and enjoying a little side treat.

It was easy to run upon the reef, but to get off was another matter, especially with a falling tide. The motor churned the water, but at first seemed to make no impression. Even when all the boys went aft, so as to lighten the bow, there was no release.

"Something's holding her, I tell you! It may be one of those octopus fish we hear so much about," suggested Will.

Jerry, who had been pulling on a pair of heavy old shoes, with the intention of going overboard, so as to put his shoulder to the bow, and lifting while the motor worked, looked a little dubious.

"Humbug! Can't be any such thing, eh, Frank?" he asked, turning to the one in whose opinion he always felt the most implicit faith.

"What's holding her is that ridge of 'coon oysters. They grip like all creation, Joe, here, says. Wait till I get some old shoes on, Jerry, and I'll be with you," he observed.

Presently both of them were over in the water, which only came to their knees.

"Ready, now, Will. When I say the word, turn on all speed astern. How about it, pard?" Frank said to Jerry.

"Right, here," came the reply.

"Then go!"

After the motor started working, the two in the water lifted. Just as Frank had anticipated, the thing was easy. Back went the *Jessamine* with a rush; indeed, Jerry was not quick enough in trying to draw himself aboard, and they left him there, marooned on the 'coon oyster bar.

"Hi, you! Come back here after me! Think I'm Bluff, and want a mortgage on the whole blooming bed, don't you? Shove me the little dinghy, if you're afraid of scratching more of the varnish off Cousin Archie's boat!" he shouted.

"Hold on! Please wait! I want to get a picture of him standing there in the big bay, just as if he owned the sea. It's Neptune, coming out of the water, you know," called Will beseechingly.

So Jerry felt constrained to humor the artist, and assume a position that, according to Will's idea, accorded with his condition of lonesomeness.

"I think we'll just pole along, fellows, and not run the motor. I guess we don't want to go very far in, anyhow, for we'll have the dickens of a time getting out again in the morning," remarked Frank.

"There's some sort of a shack over yonder on the mainland," remarked Will.

Frank took a look.

"Possibly the place where some of those turtlers put up when out after their game. They keep the green turtles in what they call a 'crawl,' until ready to set sail for Cedar Keys. I'm told we'll see lots of them there," remarked Frank.

"I can see an old boat drawn up on shore, but not the first sign of life about the place. There's a buzzard sitting on a dead tree - yes, a row of 'em! My! I hope there ain't anybody dead in there!"

Will had brought out Frank's marine glasses, and was looking through them as he gave utterance to this forlorn expression.

"Oh! let up on that, Will! You give a fellow the creeps. Just why should there be any one dead yonder? Buzzards are found everywhere in Florida, millions of 'em. I reckon the shack is deserted. To prove it, I'm going to paddle over and see, just as soon as we get fast to our mudhook again," remarked Jerry.

"And that will be right now," said Frank. "Give it a toss, Bluff. Here we seem to be in a little spot deeper than the rest of the bayou, and with room to swing around with a change of wind without fouling our anchor or going aground again on any miserable oyster bed."

"Look here! I've got a grievance," remarked Bluff.

"All right. Let's hear it," laughed Will.

"If he takes the dinghy, how in the world am I going to gather the oysters for our supper? Frank said the very next mess we got he would give us scalloped oysters, and I'm just feeling hungry that way," complained Bluff.

"Oh, don't worry. I'll be back in half an hour, at the most. Besides, if you want to, you can put on these heavy shoes of mine, drop over the side, and wade to the bar. It's warm in the water, and delightful," remarked Jerry, slipping over into the small boat, with his rifle in his hand.

"Well, there's no depending on you. Half an hour, did you say? More than likely that means about dark, if there's any temptation to hunt ashore. So I suppose I'll just have to duck, and do the great wading act. For I count it next door to a crime to be so near delicious oysters and not have them at least once a day."

Bluff was as good as his word. He put on the heavy shoes, and some old garments. Then, getting a bucket, he crept overboard, found that the water only came to his waist, and, having marked out his course, was speedily on a reef, digging at the largest oysters he could find.

"Boys, they're just the finest ever! Some whoppers out here, too. No 'coon oyster about that chap," and he held up one that was half again as large as his hand.

Now and then, as he worked, they could see him stop to try an extra fat-looking fellow. When this had been repeated a dozen times, Will reproached him.

"Where do we come in? Do we get the culls?" he demanded.

"Why, hang it, my bucket's as full now as it will hold! I'm coming across to dump 'em on the deck, and get another helping. Why, I could keep at this business all day. It's just fascinating, that's what!" called Bluff.

"I see your finish, all right, my fine boy. You'll never go back to Centerville again. Either you'll turn into an oyster, after devouring so many tons of 'em, or else hire out to the owner of a sharpie engaged in the business," laughed Frank.

He had to admit, though, when Bluff opened one of the big fellows and allowed him a chance to taste its flavor, that they were the best he had ever run across.

"Barring none," declared Bluff vigorously, holding the oyster knife aloft.

"Barring none," affirmed Frank, also erecting his fingers, as though willing to go on record.

Then, of course, Will had to try them, also, and also frankly pronounced them delicious.

"Let me have that knife, Bluff, and I'll be opening some while you're off after another supply. The hatchet will be all you want to loosen any tight ones. Don't look at me that way. I can be trusted not to eat more than one in five. And my appetite for oysters isn't one-third what yours is," laughed Frank.

Bluff seemed to think he could stand that, for he yielded up the opener.

"Don't you let that scoffer, Will, have another one. I'll bring back another bucketful in about ten minutes. There's millions of 'em. They set me wild to think of such riches going to waste. I'll dream about 'em, fellows."

Grumbling thus, he stalked through the water to the reef, and set to work again.

Frank had watched Jerry push in to shore and vanish among the tangled undergrowth. Some little time had passed since, but there was no sign of his returning.

"I guess it's lucky Bluff didn't take his word for it, and wait," he remarked.

"Yes," replied Will, who was watching the fat bivalves drop into the kettle as his chum deftly manipulated the opening knife, "I rather think we'd have missed connections with this savory mess, all right, and all of us would have been sorry."

"I wonder if he found anybody in that old shack?" mused Frank, looking again.

"Hardly likely. What would you say, Joe? Ever been ashore here?"

The boy shook his head in the negative.

"Not me. This is my first trip up this far. Been down the coast, below Cedar Keys, more'n once. But I believe Jerry likes to hunt. Perhaps he might think it a good time to look around, and see if there happens to be a deer waiting to be cooked up."

Frank laughed.

"You've got Jerry sized up to a pretty fine point, boy. That's his weakness to a dot, and I wouldn't put it past him to wander off. I only hope he doesn't go and get lost. That would delay us, even if nothing worse came of it"

"There!"

As Will made this utterance there came the sharp report of a gun from the mainland, and undoubtedly the rifle was that of their absent chum.

"Wonder what he's struck now?" said Frank.

There came two more reports, in quick succession.

Bluff was already hastening in from the oyster bar, staggering under his load.

"Hey! D'ye hear all that shooting, fellows? Jerry's in some sort of trouble, I'll bet my hat!" he shouted excitedly.

"And we are unable to get ashore, for he has the only boat, and the water is too shallow to push the big craft in. The question is, what shall we do?"

Frank looked into the faces of his two chums, and saw by their increasing pallor that they more than shared the fears that were beginning to gnaw at his heart in connection with the safety of the genial, good-natured Jerry Wallington.

CHAPTER XIX

WHAT HAPPENED TO JERRY

"I'd give something for a pair of wings just now!" exclaimed Will regretfully.

"Or that bally old balloon of Professor Smythe's, eh?" echoed Bluff, as he surveyed the stretch of water separating them from the mainland.

"But something *must* be done! Bluff, get your gun!"

Frank was hastily removing the tennis shoes he wore aboard the boat.

"What're you going to do?" demanded Will, as Bluff made haste to obey.

"Two of us must get ashore. Perhaps Jerry needs help."

"Oh! I see! And you think you can wade there?" queried Will, as he saw Frank drawing on the second pair of heavy shoes, that had already been in the water.

"That's what we have to do. Ready, Bluff?" cried Frank, snatching up his own double-barreled shotgun.

"Where do I come in?" demanded Will as they slid overboard.

"You're the goalkeeper this time. Hold the ship, with Joe, here, till we get back."

"And they've taken all the guns along," grumbled Will as he watched his two chums making their splashing way in the direction of the shore.

Happening to bethink himself of the old revolver on board, Will presently armed himself with the same, and tried to imagine that he presented an imposing appearance as the guardian of the motor-boat. Truth to tell, he would have really been far more dangerous handling his favorite camera, for he did not have it in him to harm a flea, if he could help it.

Meanwhile, Frank and his comrade were pushing for the shore as rapidly as the conditions allowed. By exercising a certain amount of discretion they were able to follow up one of the oyster reefs that thrust out from the bank like the fingers of a human hand.

"We'll make it all right," declared Bluff presently.

"Yes, and without getting in deeper than half way up. But I'm wondering why we don't hear anything more from Jerry. He had six charges in his rifle, you know."

From Frank's tone it was easy to understand that he was worried.

"Say, perhaps that was meant for a signal," suggested Bluff suddenly.

"There were three shots, just as we've always agreed, but then they were scattered somewhat. I hardly agree with you, Bluff, though it may be true. I hope it is, and yet Jerry must have known we had no boat. He would hardly want us to come ashore unless he was in a mighty serious pickle."

"Anyhow, we're nearly there, and must soon know the worst,"

said Bluff, whose face looked a bit peaked under the suspense.

More through accident than design, they landed close to the spot where the old palmetto shack could be seen. Frank pointed to an enclosure along the edge of the bayou, made by piling up logs and pieces of coquina rock.

"Turtle crawl," he said, as they hurried past, and Bluff only gave it one look, for his attention was taken up with the more serious matter that had brought them ashore.

Advancing to the shack, Frank looked in, but there did not appear to be a living soul around.

He surveyed his surroundings with anxiety. Great live-oaks, with their crooked limbs covered with the trailing Spanish moss; tall palmettos, and shorter young ones of the same type; gumbo-limbo trees, wild plum, and several wild orange trees, made up the immediate surroundings.

"Oh! if we only had some idea which way he could have gone!" exclaimed Frank.

"Perhaps he left a trail," was the bright thought of Bluff.

"Almost impossible to map it out in this black sand," Frank replied; but, nevertheless, he started to look, since there was nothing else to do.

A dozen impossible things flashed through Frank's brain as he bent over to try and pick up the tracks of his missing chum. Whatever could have happened to Jerry? Usually he was able to take good care of himself; could it be possible that some inmate of the dilapidated shack had stolen upon him, bent upon robbery? In that case, how account for the shots?

"Let's shout," said Bluff again.

"A bright thought, and surely it can do no harm. Let me call singly, Bluff."

Thereupon Frank lifted up his voice and shouted:

"Jerry! Jerry! Where are you?"

The call rang through the thick jungle under the live-oaks. A small animal, possibly a 'coon, scurried through the undergrowth. In an adjacent tree a Florida bluejay gave forth a discordant scream. A fox-squirrel barked saucily, and with a flirt of his bushy tail scrambled around to the other side of a hickory tree.

Then came a shout that thrilled them:

"Ahoy, there, Frank!"

"It's Jerry!" cried Bluff, ready to throw his hat into the air.

Frank himself was tremendously relieved. No matter what had happened, their chum was alive, and could call to them.

"Hello! What's the matter? Where are you?" he shouted, for the voice of Jerry had come from a little distance away, and seemed strangely muffled.

"Straight into the woods from the shack!" came back the reply.

"We're coming to you!" called Frank, still puzzled to know what it all meant.

"I wonder what he has dropped into now?" speculated Bluff as he trotted along at the heels of his leader.

"Sounds as if he wanted us to come to him, all right. Keep your gun ready, Bluff, for there's no telling but what you may need it," Frank went on.

"It's in apple-pie shape for business at the old stand. Jerry laughs at it, but before now he's found that it could help a fellow out of a hole. Suppose you try him again?"

Bluff's suggestion was a good one, and Frank raised his voice in a shout. This time the answer came from a point closer at hand. Still, although they were peering eagerly through the dense foliage, they could see nothing out of the way.

"This beats the Dutch! Where under the sun can the fellow be?" said Bluff, after they had gone still further.

"What's that?" asked Frank suddenly, pointing.

"I declare if it doesn't look some like a dead deer, a little fellow, too; perhaps a fawn," came from Bluff as he hurried forward.

"No, it's a full-grown deer, all right, and just killed, too. They run very small down here, you know. But that doesn't tell us where our chum is, even if he shot the game, and had to fire three times in order to down it," declared Frank.

"As sure as you live, here's his gun!" cried Bluff.

Frank stared at the rifle, that lay at the foot of a particularly big live-oak, parts of which seemed to be rotting away, as there were dead limbs strewing the ground underneath it. Then he cast his eyes upward, as if under the impression that he might discover Jerry perched upon a limb, laughing at them.

"He isn't up there. I've examined every limb on the old tree. What under the sun do you suppose could have happened to him?" ejaculated Bluff.

"Hark!" said Frank, holding up his hand.

"He's laughing at us! I tell you that was Jerry's chuckle, for all the world! Now, what tomfoolery is he up to, do you suppose? Bringing us ashore through all that beastly water just to have a shy at us! Hi, Jerry, you old joker! Show up!" cried Bluff indignantly.

The only answer was a second laugh, louder than the first.

"I declare he's up in that blessed tree, after all, and yet for the life of me I can't get a squint at him. Serve the old chap right if we went and took the dinghy back, leaving him to wade," grumbled Bluff.

Frank was looking around him. He noticed several little things just then. Among others was the fact that there were scratches on the bark of the big old oak, as though some one might have scrambled up its trunk recently. An air-plant lay on the ground, evidently detached during the progress of that party.

"I'm beginning to smell a rat," Frank said, slowly.

"Then let me in, please. I'm just devoured with curiosity to know what it all means," pleaded his chum.

"Listen! Don't you hear a strange buzzing up there?" demanded Frank.

"Now that you mention it, I believe I do. Sounds to me like a hive of bees."

"That's just what it is, and Jerry knew it as soon as he heard it. A hive of bees in this old live-oak, with perhaps a big store of honey laid up. Bluff, doesn't that tickle your palate? Well, it did Jerry's, for sure. He climbed up!"

"After he had shot that deer, then?" asked Bluff.

"Undoubtedly. I remember, now, that honey always appealed to Jerry more than any other sweet stuff. He was remarking, only the last time we had flapjacks, that it was a beastly blunder we had none of us thought to bring a bottle of honey along."

"But he isn't up there, now, for I can see the whole tree. Still he keeps on chuckling. I can't make it out, Frank. But you know, for I see it in your face! Where is Jerry?"

Frank deliberately rapped on the trunk of the big oak.

"Hello, Jerry! Anybody at home in there?" he called.

"Only a stranger and a pilgrim, who wants to get out the worst way, and can't," came in a muffled voice.

Bluff gave a roar of amazement.

"Why, he's inside the tree!" he ejaculated.

"Just what he is. Stepped on some punky, rotten wood above there, that must have given way under his weight, and our fine chum shot down into the hollow trunk of the big king," laughed Frank.

"Correct, Frank. Just how it happened. I've tried again and again to climb up to that hole where I came in, but the plagued walls are too slippery, and I fell back every time. Please mount the tree, and lower a coat or something for me to get a grip on," came in muffled tones to their ears.

Both Frank and Bluff rolled upon the ground with shrieks of laughter. If the sounds of their merriment carried to the ears of Will, he must have been greatly mystified as to the cause of the same.

But Jerry was getting impatient.

"Hurry up, and get to work! It ain't over nice in here, I tell you," he called; and so the two climbed up the tree to effect his rescue.

Bluff had a coat, so they lowered that by a sleeve, stretching down as far as possible. Jerry managed to scramble up far enough to lay hold on the other sleeve, and was, after one or two efforts, assisted to the opening. He came out looking a bit dilapidated, yet just as determined as ever to get some of that honey before leaving the vicinity.

The others were not averse to laying in a supply of the same, and promised to arrange it for the morning, for night was now close at hand, and nothing could be done looking to an attack upon the bee tree.

They carried the doe down to the water's edge. Jerry had come upon the animal soon after entering among the trees, and she had startled him by her sudden jump, so that it took three shots from his rifle to drop her. Then, as he stood over his game, the buzzing of the bees had attracted his attention, as the late comers arrived, laden with honey; and unable to resist the inclination to investigate, he had climbed up, with the disastrous result as stated.

Bluff and Frank waded out to the motor-boat, allowing Jerry to ferry his venison in the little dinghy. Will greeted their coming with delight, for he saw great possibilities for future feasts in the game acquired.

Of course he was wild to hear the story, which was told amid much merriment all around while they dined off fresh venison steak and scalloped oysters.

CHAPTER XX

LYING IN AMBUSH FOR BIG GAME

"Nobody lives in that old shack, then?" inquired Will.

"Only when the turtle season is on, which doesn't happen to be now," replied Frank.

"I was afraid there might be a bunch of criminals ashore, and that Jerry had tumbled into a peck of trouble," continued the other.

"Oh, it happened to be only a hollow tree he dropped into," said the hero of the adventure, who could take a joke even when it happened to be on himself.

"There it goes again! Just think what beastly luck! I'm a Jonah, that's what! Oh! why didn't you ask me to go, instead of Bluff, Frank? I could have snapped him off when he was crawling out of that hole. Just think what a lovely reminder it would have been in times to come!" wailed Will, pretending to be bitterly disappointed, though Frank imagined he was assuming this to tantalize Jerry.

"Talk to me about your artistic temperament! What d'ye call that? Me crawling out of that old bee tree make a beautiful picture! Yes, I guess it might, for the rest of you, but I'm satisfied to let the episode die a natural death. But wait till we fill up our spare pots and pans with that delicious honey! Um!

um!" And Jerry smacked his lips as he contemplated the feast in store.

They spent the night quietly enough. Nothing occurred to bother them, save the one annoyance they experienced from sandflies. The tiny creatures attacked them as soon as the breeze died out, and for an hour or two proved irritating in the extreme.

Bluff executed a war dance as he slapped at his invisible persecutors, and wondered if he were going into a fever, his face and neck and arms burned so. Luckily, a night breeze coming up, drove the horde of tiny insects away, but for several days the boys were rubbing and scratching at the irritated skin.

"'Skeeters ain't in it with the little pests!" vowed Jerry, and the whole party seemed to be of the same opinion.

After an early breakfast they made preparations looking to a raid on the rich stores of the bee tree. An old piece of netting was made into nets, so as to cover their faces, while gloves protected their hands fairly well.

Jerry took them ashore, all but Bluff, who elected to stay by the boat. The others jeered him, and declared that he was afraid of stings; but Bluff was not to be taunted into going.

Joe, who had been up a bee tree before, offered to ascend, and do the work. So the balance of the party were only too glad of the chance to escape that duty.

The hive was in a big limb that jutted out just above where Jerry had crashed through a rotten place marking the spot where another limb had broken off long years before.

"It looks easy. I reckon I can chop her some, and she'll drop of her own weight," called the boy.

He began to use the small camp ax with telling effect. After half an hour of this there was an ominous crack.

"Look sharp, down there! She's a-comin'!" called Joe.

Hardly had he spoken than the limb came down with a roar. Instantly the air was filled with a swarm of thousands of dazed bees. The limb had split open from the concussion, and a wonderful store of honey was displayed to view. Jerry was wild with delight.

"Gallons and gallons of the lovely stuff!" he shouted. "Come on, fellows, and get the pails filled! Ouch! That little imp got me, all right! Say! he's inside my veil! Whoop! There's another! I must have left an opening!" And for a minute or so he danced around madly, slapping and pawing, until he had managed to dispose of the furious insects.

By the time he had adjusted his net the others were busy at work.

"Take only the lighter-colored honey. That dark stuff is old, though I suppose it's all good still. We can't use a fifth of what there is. I imagine I know what will happen around here to-night," said Frank.

Joe looked up and grinned.

"Bear come, sure. Smell the honey a mile away," he remarked, and Frank nodded.

"And if we were wild to get a bear, all we'd have to do would be to sit here and wait," remarked Will, who had, of course, snapped off a few views while his chums were busy, particularly remembering Jerry while he pranced around and fought the busy bees that had invaded his head net.

"I leave that to the rest," remarked Frank.

Having secured all the honey they could carry away, they once more returned to the shore, and by degrees their sweet cargo was ferried out to the motor-boat. Of course, more or less washing up followed, for they were all sticky.

"What is it to be, fellows - go, or stay over?" asked Frank a little later.

Bluff had been told about the chances for bagging a bear, but he did not seem to care much about it.

"I say go on," he remarked indifferently.

"Bear for me," declared Jerry.

"How about you, Will?" asked Frank.

"Oh, I'm with Bluff this time. If it was in the daytime, now, and I thought I could get a picture of the shoot, I might look at it differently."

"You happen to have run out of flashlight cartridges, then? That's too bad! Well, I side with Jerry," remarked Frank, smiling.

"But that makes it a tie. We'll have to toss for it, fellows," came from Will.

"You forget Joe, here. Let him cast the deciding vote. How, Joe?"

The boy grinned, and looked affectionately at Frank.

"I like bear steak," he said simply.

"Hurrah! That settles it, then!" shouted Jerry.

They just loafed through that day.

"Take it easy, boys. Strenuous times may be ahead of us yet. Who knows? Besides, we are doing finely. Half the time gone, and we're surely more than half way along our journey, counting the river trip. We can easily spare the day." And Frank set each to amusing himself after his own particular fashion.

Jerry went in the dinghy to try the fishing where the water was deeper, and it was not half an hour before they heard him yelling with delight as his little shallop was being towed around this way and that by a fish.

"Another shark! He'd better cut loose!" exclaimed Will, in some alarm.

Joe shook his head.

"No shark this time. I think he has got fast to a big channel bass. It runs and then stops, then runs again. Shark keeps on all the while," he explained.

It proved to be the case, for when Jerry came back he proudly exhibited a monster bronze-backed prize that must have weighed more than thirty pounds.

Of course it was hung up, and a picture taken, with the gallant victor in the contest standing alongside, stout rod in hand.

So the evening came at last, and they turned their thoughts to big game.

Will and Bluff were elected to remain on board, as a penance for having voted against staying over.

"We'll stand for that, all right; but if you should keel over a Bruin, don't you fellows think we're going to let you fool us out of our share of the prog," said Bluff.

It took two trips of the dinghy to land the three hunters. Of course, Joe had only gone along to see the fun, for he had no gun.

Still, he was capable of advancing some good suggestions, calculated to be of value to them while lying in ambush for the expected bear. It was to be expected, for instance, that Bruin would make his appearance from the dense thicket beyond the bee tree, so the boys hid themselves in a semicircle, with the broken honey storehouse in plain view.

A fire had been started at a little distance, for otherwise they must have been in absolute darkness. Joe said a little thing like that would not keep the bear from coming after he had gotten a good whiff of the powerful odor of sweetness that filled the air.

The bees had been hard at work carrying a portion of their store to some new hive, but there were gallons of it still there. Everything was smeared with the sticky substance, and Frank felt sure that if a bear existed within miles of the spot that odor would be a magnet to draw the animal straight to the spot.

Talking was positively prohibited, and all the boys could do was to sit as still as the hovering mosquitoes would allow, and watch.

Once or twice, Frank thought he heard a slight rustling somewhere near. It was not what a lumbering bear would be apt to make, however, and he concluded that in all probability it must be caused by prowling 'coons.

For the third time he felt positive that his ear had caught a sound, as of a stealthy movement. To his surprise, it seemed to come from the tree under which he had taken up his station. So he naturally bent his head back in the effort to locate the little animal that must be curiously observing him.

A thrill passed through his frame as he first of all caught sight of two yellow eyes that glared at him not more than ten feet above his head. Then he could make out a dark body, about five feet in length, and with something moving back and forth at its extreme end.

Frank caught his breath, and his hands clutched the gun he held. He did not need any one to tell him that he was gazing up at a panther, crouching overhead, and possibly getting ready to leap down upon him at any second!

CHAPTER XXI

A STRENUOUS NIGHT

Fortunately, Frank was a quick-witted boy.

He had his gun held in such a position that it required only a simple movement to swing it upward. To aim, under the conditions, was out of the question. He had to depend entirely upon guesswork, or what might be called intuition.

Imagine the astonishment of the others, crouching close by, when a flash of flame pierced the darkness, and the crash of Frank's gun was instantly followed by a fierce scream in which both pain and fury were mingled!

Frank had no sooner fired than he threw himself backward. Knowing something about the habits of these animals, he understood that the panther would make its leap, no matter how seriously it might be wounded.

Frank did not claim to be an acrobat, but he certainly made a record for himself in the line of back tumbling.

"Who shot?" shouted Jerry in amazement.

"Where's the bear?" came from Joe, equally amazed and confused.

Frank had by this time managed to scramble to his feet. He

was somewhat scratched, and would perhaps feel a bit sore from his tremendous effort, but his heart beat high with anticipation when he realized that all was still in the quarter where he had been snugly lying.

"Stir up the fire, Jerry, and fetch a torch here!" he called, holding himself in readiness for another shot, if such should be needed.

"You just bet I will!" cried the other, bounding forward.

Frank saw him give the smoldering fire a kick that started it into new life. Then, bending over, he snatched a brand and came running back.

"Where are you, Frank? What under the sun happened? Not hurt, are you?" was what he was singing out, his voice trembling with eagerness and anxiety.

"Everything all right, Jerry. Come this way. Now poke the blaze over yonder."

Jerry gave a shout.

"Something's moving! It's kicking its last, by the great horn spoon! Frank's got his bear - no, I'll be hanged if it is! A panther, Joe, a panther!"

He stood there like a statue, holding the torch and staring at the sleek gray form stretched out under the tree, and which was, in fact, giving the very last kick, as he had declared.

Frank laughed, a little hysterically, it may be assumed, for the strain on his nerves had been tremendous.

"Unexpected visitor, eh, Jerry? Didn't send out an invitation to this slippery gentleman, did we? But he insisted on joining the family circle, and I just *had* to ask him in," he said, trying to steady his voice, while, unseen by Jerry, his hands were shaking as he clutched his gun.

"Tell me about that, will you! Oh, yes, he came, all right. That was a warm invitation he couldn't resist. But how did you see him, Frank? Where was the sly old cat? Say! he must have jumped for you, I guess, for that was just where you were squatting!"

Frank shuddered as he saw that this was true. Only for his quick action in vacating his position he must have been torn by the poisonous claws of the dying beast.

"He was sitting just above my head, on that limb there," he remarked quietly.

"Talk to me about your cute ones, what could equal that? Do you think the old slinker was there all the time?" demanded Jerry, shaking his head.

"Oh, no. That is out of the question. Our coming must have alarmed him if he had been so close by. I imagine he crept through the trees while we lay here waiting, like so many mummies."

"I say, Frank, do panthers like honey?" demanded the other.

"Well, now, you've got me there. Never having had any experience in that line, I'm in the dark. How about it, Joe?" laughed Frank.

"I never heard of one that did. S'pect he was snoopin' around to see what we was a-doin' here. Then there was the smell of the blood from the deer, you know," explained the Florida boy wisely.

"Why, of course! That's it. But I say, Frank, do we cut out the bear hunt now?"

"That's for you to say. I've had my shot, but if you're satisfied to stay, why, count on me to keep you company."

"I had my heart set on bear steak. The only thing is, will old Bruin come now, after all this rumpus?" said Jerry disconsolately.

"If half that I've heard about his liking for wild honey is true, a dozen rackets like that couldn't keep him away. Joe, you know. Tell us if that isn't so?" asked Frank.

"Oh, he'll come, all right, if he smells that honey," returned the boy confidently.

"That settles it, then. We stay a while, at any rate," declared Frank.

Jerry was secretly pleased. Perhaps he did have a little streak of envy in his composition, for it galled him to have others succeed in his beloved sport while fortune denied him a fair share of the honors. But, taken all in all, Jerry was square enough, and would quickly change places with a companion in a boat when it appeared that all the fish were lying at his end.

Frank moved his position a little. Then they settled down to wait. Of course, every one of the three boys cast rather frequent and apprehensive glances up into the branches overhead. Sometimes these panthers hunted in pairs, and how were they to tell but what the mate to Frank's victim might be even then watching for a chance to leap down upon them?

An hour passed. Then Jerry heard a grunting sound somewhere close by. It was accompanied by a rustling in the bushes.

His pulses thrilled, while Joe, who had taken up a position alongside him after the adventure with the panther, put out a hand and nudged Jerry several times.

"Bear!" he said, in the lowest of whispers.

Again and again came the grunting and the swishing of bushes. Bruin was sniffing the delightful aroma of honey. It was so strong that his usual caution was apparently thrown to the winds, and he pushed forward straight toward the spot where the broken tree hive had scattered much of its delicious contents over the ground.

Now Jerry could see his bulky figure as he shuffled forward with eager mien. The repeating rifle began to come up, though Jerry was in no hurry to fire. He wanted to get a fair view of the animal's side, so that he could bring Bruin down with a single shot.

They could hear the beast grunting in delight as he started in to devour some of the bees' rich treasure. Perhaps he had long cast an envious eye on that same tree hive, and hoped for the time to come when a storm might lay it low.

Frank held his fire generously. He could have shot the bear several times, and with the buckshot shells that were in his gun had no fear about killing his game with ease; but it was really Jerry's turn.

Finally came the sharp report. They saw the bear roll over, try to stagger up again, struggle vehemently, and then gradually grow weaker.

"Hurrah, Jerry! He's your bag!" shouted Frank, as genuinely happy as though it had been his own shot that did the business; perhaps more so.

"Oh! what a night! Bring on your bears and panthers, your crocodiles and tomcats!" cried Jerry. "We can take care of a whole menagerie. Talk to me about your hunting preserves! Did you ever meet up with anything that equals this?"

Realizing that the boys on board the motorboat must be consumed with eagerness to know what the result of these two shots might be, Frank now proposed that they go aboard.

"We want some sleep, you see. In the morning we'll be able to attend to these fellows. I guess nothing will bother them until then," he said.

He and Joe entered the little dinghy, and it was ferried across the water to the anchored boat. There they were met by both Will and Bluff, who, being aroused by the first shot, had sat there, swathed in blankets, watching for the return of the mighty Nimrods.

"What luck?" called Bluff, evidently repenting that he had not accompanied them.

"Oh, Jerry got his bear, all right," sang out Frank indifferently, while he kept on pushing the smaller boat closer to the other.

"But didn't you shoot? Will declared it was your shotgun that awoke us first - it must have been hours ago," went on Bluff curiously.

"Why, yes. I had a shot at a gray visitor who threatened to jump down on me from the tree." And Frank began climbing aboard so that Joe could go back after the other chum.

"What! Do you mean a panther?" burst out Bluff.

"Sure! Wait till you see the chap, in the morning. Looks like a dandy," replied Frank, trying to appear unconcerned.

"Then you got him?"

"It was a case of getting him before he got me." And then, taking pity on the boys, who were fairly burning with eagerness to hear, he told how he had happened to discover the crouching beast that had crept into the tree without their knowledge.

Presently Jerry came aboard. Both of the hunters, as well as young Joe, were too sleepy for further conversation.

"You'll see it all in the morning. And Will, we can hang up the game so that you'll have a fine shot at the scene, bee tree and all. Every time we look at it our mouths will water at the thought of all that fine honey going to waste," and with this parting remark Frank crawled under his blanket.

Nothing happened to disturb the outdoor chums during the balance of the night. With the coming of morning they were astir. Breakfast was a hurried meal. Then they went ashore in detachments, Joe remaining behind to look after the boat.

Will managed to get a good picture of the trophies, with the two gallant hunters standing beside the defunct bear and panther. Then, after the former had been washed, being sticky with the honey, Frank assisted Jerry to get the skin off. It was here the boys profited by the advice given by the old trapper, Jesse Wilcox, when they visited him in his camp above Rocky Creek, which was a feeder to the lake upon which their home town was located.

Before noon they were all aboard again. Both skins had been secured, besides the choice portions of the bear meat. Bluff even managed to fill another kettle with the honey, though stung unmercifully by the angry bees that were so busily working to transfer their stores to a new home.

After a bite of lunch they started out again on the gulf, since the conditions invited an afternoon cruise. Frank knew they would find a good holding place not more than twenty miles further along the shore, and he aimed to reach it before the coming of night.

It was just four o'clock when they pushed in behind another key and made their way to the mainland, for here the water was quite deep.

"I move for a camp ashore, for a change," suggested Jerry.

"Second that motion. My back's nearly broken from these

hard boards," grunted Bluff. "Oh, dear! If we only had our air mattresses along, Frank!"

"Yes, if we only had!" exclaimed Jerry. "Then you'd soon quit claiming that you had bigger lungs than I've got. You know I beat you in blowing up my bag."

"Yes, just once more than I came in winner. Isn't that so, Frank?"

Frank poured oil on the troubled waters, but he and Will winked at each other, for the joke always amused them.

They erected the tent, and had their jolly campfire, which reminded them of many in the past. It was, of course, thought a good thing to secure the boat with chain and padlock, so that no prowling scamp could make off with it while they slept, for they meant to keep no watch.

Joe found a place on board, as there was no room in the tent. Besides, he had not a temperament that delighted in such things, and would only too gladly have always felt sure of having a good roof over him at night.

The four boys were a bit crowded. Still, they joked over the thing as they settled down, and after a time only the glow of the still burning fire told that human beings were somewhere near by.

They slept soundly, despite the close quarters, since the air was cool, and, for a wonder, no mosquitoes worried them. Those who were dreaming must have imagined the end of the world had suddenly arrived, for the tent was, without the least warning, knocked down, leaving the four amazed boys scrambling and shouting under the canvas, and trying to crawl out from the wreckage.

CHAPTER XXII

THE MESSAGE FROM THE AIR

"What struck us?" And Bluff poked his head out from under the canvas, looking for all the world like a tortoise, Frank thought, as he followed suit.

"Tell me about that, will you! Where's the villain who cut the ropes? I can whip him with one hand!" panted Jerry, struggling in a mess of camp necessities, and kicking around among the aluminum ware that Frank prized so highly.

"Where's my camera? Some fellow has run off with my camera!" wailed Will.

By this time Frank had extricated himself from the wreckage and began to assist the others to regain their feet. No one seemed to be seriously injured, and the mystery was great. What had happened to smash down their tent in that strange way?

"The ropes were never cut, fellows!" announced Bluff, after a hasty examination.

"Something *fell* on us, that's what!" observed Jerry, shaking that wise head of his in his obstinate fashion as he surveyed the ruins of the tent.

Frank seized upon the idea quickly.

"I believe you've struck the truth, Jerry!" he exclaimed.

"Then it must have been a shooting-star or a piece off a comet," said Will.

"Not much. I am sure I heard voices calling out, and laughing over the joke. I tell you somebody's playing a nasty trick on us, that's what!" declared Bluff.

"Voices, did you say? Are you sure?" demanded Frank, stopping in his fumbling around the tent, while Jerry was throwing some dead palmetto leaves on the fire to induce a speedy blaze, so that they might have more light.

"Yes, I'm sure; and they were out there, too," continued Bluff, pointing beyond the motor-boat.

"I heard 'em, too!" called Joe, at this juncture, as his head appeared in view above the combing of the craft.

"Out on the bayou?" asked Frank, anxious to solve the strange mystery.

"Sure! And there was something like the creaking of sails, too. But I don't think they was makin' fun of us. I kinder thought one of 'em called out somethin' that sounded like, 'Help us!'" went on Joe breathlessly.

"Talk to me about your mysteries! Who ever ran up against a worse one than this?" gasped Jerry, scratching his head, as he shivered in the cool air.

"What time is it, anyhow?" demanded Will, who had now found his camera, and was feeling satisfied, because it did not appear to have sustained any injury.

"Time? I declare if that isn't dawn in the east, fellows! Time we were up, I guess," remarked Frank, stooping over again, determined to learn the secret of the sudden and violent collapse of the tent, accompanied by such strange whispering voices that seemed to die away in the distance.

"Well, all I can say is that if dawn comes with such a swoop down in this blessed country, it's me back to my native heath again," grumbled Jerry, who had received a few bruises in the mix-up. Up to now he had paid no attention to them, but they were beginning to make themselves manifest.

"What's this?"

Frank uttered the cry as he bent over and stared at something which he had discovered under the canvas.

"Hold on! I've got my gun handy!" exclaimed Bluff, thinking that if it were a wild animal his time had come to distinguish himself.

"Oh! What is it?" echoed Will, crowding near.

The fire was now leaping madly up as the tinder-like dried palmetto leaves and stalks caught, so that every one could easily see.

"Why, it's a bag! - a big bean bag!" exclaimed Will, in amazement. "Where, in the name of goodness, did that come from, fellows?"

"A bean bag! Tell me about that, will you?" said Jerry. And then, as he bent over to clutch hold of it, he went on: "Why, as sure as you live, it's a *sand bag*! Who ever could have shied that thing at us and then run away?"

Frank was more than startled. He had seen just such bags before, and filled with sand, too. He knew to what uses they were put.

"Say! What do you think, that bag is ballast from a balloon or airship?" he cried.

"Ballast!"

"From an airship!"

The four outdoor chums stood there and stared, first at each other and then at the suspicious bag that lay there on the canvas. There could be no mistake about its contents, for one seam had broken, and the sand was trickling out even now.

"Then a balloon passed over us in the night, and they threw out a sand bag to lighten her! What do you think of that?" gasped Jerry, as if hardly able to grasp the strangeness of the affair.

"Why would they want to lighten her?" asked Bluff.

Frank was quick to perceive facts.

"Listen, fellows! Joe, here, says the voices were out yonder, toward the key, and that they gradually grew less distinct. That would happen, you know, if a balloon were gradually drifting out toward the open gulf."

"Tell me about that, now! Do you really think they were being run away with?" asked Jerry in a tense tone, as he tried to picture the alarm that must overwhelm aeronauts under such conditions.

"Didn't Joe say he was sure he heard some one cry out, 'Help us'? Wouldn't that indicate danger for the balloonists? I tell you what, boys, this was the most remarkable thing that ever happened to us. To think that the sand bag, and maybe an anchor, knocked our tent down with a smash, and didn't kill or seriously injure a single one of us beats the record! But I'm sorry for those fellows, though."

"So am I, Frank. I wish we could do something to help them," remarked Will.

"Couldn't we put out right away? They may fall into the gulf any minute, and be drowned! Say! Why not go, Frank?" pursued Jerry.

"Get some clothes on, the first thing, fellows. We're not going back to bed again now, anyway. The dawn is surely coming on, and we could get out on the gulf in a short time, if we concluded to try it."

They had left their outer garments aboard the motor-boat, so that it was easy enough to find them now. Hastily they dressed, all the while chattering like a lot of magpies. But it might have been noticed that every one was in favor of doing something to assist the drifting balloonists, who had apparently gone out to sea in a helpless airship.

Frank was dressed a little before any of the rest. Something seemed to have come into his mind, for he hurried ashore again, as if bent upon examining the sand bag once more.

"What's he up to?" asked Bluff, for the daylight was now growing strong enough for them to see to some extent.

"Wants to look at that bean bag of Will's again, I guess. Perhaps he thinks we may have a good supper off the contents," jeered Jerry.

"Now I think he expects to get a clue, somehow. Perhaps there may be a name sewed on the old bag. Seems to me, balloonists do that, so the people below may report their passing over, especially when there's a race on," remarked Will calmly.

"And that's just what he's up to," declared Bluff, "for you see he's turning the bag over now. There! He's struck something, by the way he grabs! It's a letter, fellows, as sure as you live!"

"A letter from the skies! Tell me about that, will you!" whistled Jerry as he bounded ashore and hurried to join Frank.

"What's doing?" he asked anxiously, as he came to where the other was standing, staring at the piece of paper he held in his hand.

"Remarkable! Who would ever have believed it?" Frank was saying.

"Well, please take pity on the rest of us, and let us have a little light," Will broke out with.

"It came from the *Kentucky*, fellows!" Frank observed, shaking his head, as if he could hardly believe his senses.

"That was the name of the balloon our good friend, Professor Jason Smythe, expected to pilot in the drift from Atlanta to Savannah, to test the air currents."

This from Jerry, who was equally amazed.

"How do you know?" asked Bluff, of course, since he never accepted anything without abundant proof.

"The name is sewed on the bag. I found it underneath. But there was something more, boys - this letter, written, with others of the same kind, and sent down in the hope that one of them might fall into the hands of some person who would notify the government station at Pensacola or Cedar Keys."

"Read it to us, Frank!"

"Yes, don't keep us in suspense. Besides, if we're going to do anything, we'd better not waste so much time here," Jerry remarked wisely.

"Then listen. Here is what it says, scribbled so that I can hardly make it out:

*   *   *   *   *

"'On board the balloon *Kentucky*, and drifting toward the gulf. Our valve refuses to work, and we dare not attempt to land in the dark. Ballast nearly gone. We fear we may be swept out to sea. Please notify station at Pensacola to send assistance - a tug, if possible. We may keep afloat a short time if we fall into the gulf.

"'JASON SMYTHE.'"

* * * * *

The boys looked awed at the remarkable coincidence of that sand bag, possibly thrown out at random, striking their tent; and they who knew the professor so well.

"But, come, fellows! We must be off! Leave these few things here till we get back. To save that daring aeronaut's life I'd sacrifice ten times as much!" cried Frank as he leaped aboard the boat and started the motor, while the others tore loose the two remaining hawsers.

CHAPTER XXIII

A DASH UPON THE GULF

"How About it, Frank? Ought all of us to go?" asked Jerry.

"Do you think any one wants to remain behind?" asked the party addressed.

"Speaking for myself, nothing could induce me to stay," came the reply.

"So say we all of us," declared Bluff, who had overheard the question.

"Besides, I think it wise that we stick together. If anything should happen that we couldn't come back here, it wouldn't matter much. You see, we've been able to tumble most of our stuff aboard in a scramble. It can be straightened out as we go. All ready, Jerry?" questioned Frank, as the other gave a shout.

"All ready! Get aboard, and start her. It's light enough to see, now. Oh! I only hope we can find the professor!" cried Jerry as he embarked.

"If Fortune is kind, we must, boys. Now we're off!"

With these words, firmly spoken, Frank opened up, and the power-boat began to move through the water. Fortunately, it was deep in this shelter, so that they could make decent speed from the beginning. Had they anchored in such a shallow bayou as their last stopping place, it must have taken an hour to get clear of the various oyster bars, running out in finger-like ridges from the shore.

Presently they cleared the point of land marking the upper end of the sheltering key, and the limitless gulf lay before them.

Morning was now rapidly advancing. The far eastern heavens had begun to take on a beautiful rosy flush, such as can be seen in no place in the wide world to better advantage than in Florida, of a winter's morning.

Every eye was instantly engaged in scouring that expanse of water, searching eagerly for a sign of the castaway balloonists. Frank even had his marine glasses leveled, and, first of all, scanned the horizon, hoping that possibly the air craft might have been able to keep afloat thus far through strenuous methods known to such a veteran sky pilot as the professor.

He was disappointed, however, for the only things that met his gaze were a few white gulls.

"What's that floating on the water over yonder, Frank?" demanded sharp-eyed Will, pointing down the coast a little.

A thrill passed through every heart. Had the lost air voyagers been sighted, and would they be rescued, after all?

Frank had his glasses focussed upon the object almost instantly.

"Too bad, fellows! Only a bunch of brown pelicans floating on the sea and waiting until breakfast time comes around," he said at once.

A chorus of remarks indicative of disappointment followed. Meantime, as the speed of the boat was rushed up to near the limit of twelve miles, and they fairly flew over the comparatively smooth gulf, each boy continued to scan the water, hoping to be the first to report success.

"How long since they passed over, do you think?" asked practical Bluff.

"I should say all of an hour," was Frank's ready response.

"One good thing, there wasn't any sort of a breeze. If it had been blowing fairly hard, the balloon would be twenty miles away by now, even if afloat."

"That's a fact Bluff; and as there wasn't an air current of more than a few miles an hour, one thing seems positive."

"What's that, Frank?" demanded Jerry.

"The balloon must have dropped into the water. If it was still in the air it could be seen through these powerful glasses miles away."

The others recognized the truth of his words.

"You seem to be heading straight out. Have you any reason for such a thing?" asked Bluff, seeking information.

"I have. Before we started I carefully noted my bearings. I also made sure that what little air was stirring came direct from the land, which, in this case, was almost due east. You can easily see from that which way the balloon must have drifted up to the minute it dragged in the water."

"Frank, what you say is sound, practical good sense. We must come on some sign in a short time, if we keep straight on and the conditions remain the same. I'm only afraid we may be too late," remarked Jerry sadly.

No one else spoke for several minutes as the motor-boat sped merrily along on her mission of mercy. It was a time of great strain. They hoped for the best, and yet were conscious of a terrible fear lest the professor and his assistant might have gone down long ere this.

"The breeze is freshening," remarked Bluff presently.

Frank had noted this, too. It was only natural, for after dawn the air currents that may have become sluggish during the night were in the habit of awakening and taking on new life.

He looked back. The land was several miles away by this time. If they were fated to meet with success in their errand, something must be showing up very soon now.

Sick at heart with apprehension, Frank handed the glasses over to Jerry, and was pretending to pay strict attention to the motor. Truth to tell, his nerves were keyed up to a high tension, as he counted the seconds, and kept hoping for the best.

Frank had noted one thing that gave him not a little concern. This was in connection with the fact that the easterly breeze seemed to have bobbed around to the southwest. Now, from all that he had heard this was a quarter that nearly always brings one of those howling "northers" that prove such a bane to Florida cruisers.

"How about that, Joe - is the fact that the wind is in the southwest apt to bring bad weather?" he asked, when he could get the cracker lad aside; for Frank did not wish to further alarm his chums.

"Most always that happens. When the wind rises now, unless she goes back once again to the south, you see she will be squally," returned Joe, also lowering his voice cautiously.

"And that squally wind develops into something stronger, I guess?" pursued the Northern boy, always seeking to learn.

"It jumps around to the northwest like a pompano skipping along the water in a shoal. Then for three days it blows like a railroad train, out of the north, and we all shiver," was the characteristic reply.

"Well, I only hope the squall part of it holds off until we pick up the poor professor. We saved him once from the fire, and now it seems up to us to pull him in out of the wet, if we have any decent sort of luck."

Noting the look of surprise on the little fellow's brown face, and realizing that he was totally ignorant in connection with what his words meant, Frank proceeded to tell how the hotel in Centerville was burned, and what a part Jerry and himself had had in the rescue of the balloonist, who had taken a sleeping powder, and lay in his room, unconscious of the tumult and peril.

Jerry meanwhile was making as good use of the marine glasses as he knew how.

"See anything that looks like the wreckage of a balloon on the water?" asked Frank, as he swept the horizon with his naked eye, but in vain.

"Not a beastly thing," returned the other, in a disappointed tone.

"Oh, I'm afraid we've come in the wrong direction," sighed tender-hearted Will, shaking his head dubiously; "and it's just terrible to think that those poor chaps may be drowning right now, and our little boat so near at hand!"

"Tell me about that, will you? There he goes as usual, making us feel like murderers or something, when we only want a chance to get in our fine rescuing act. Stop him talking that way, Frank, won't you?" pleaded Bluff, who had emptied all the sand out of the bag dropped by the drifting balloonists, and declared he meant to hang the same up in his den at home as a memento of the wonderful incident.

Frank stood up to see the better.

Carefully he scanned the horizon, beginning at the furthest possible quarter toward the south, and ranging to one equally improbable northward.

And everywhere it seemed to be the same dead level line, with not a break that gave signs of promise.

"And the strange thing about it all is that there doesn't seem to be a solitary vessel, big or little, in sight anywhere. It would be hard at any other time to find the gulf around here so utterly forsaken," he remarked, beginning to feel discouraged himself.

"It certainly looks as though we had the field to ourselves," remarked Bluff; "here we've come some miles from shore, which is getting 'hull-down,' as the sailors say, in the distance, and yet not a peep of the lost balloonists. How much further ought we go, Frank?"

"Just as long as there seems to be the slightest chance of our striking those we're looking for, or we can see shore with the glasses. I, for one, would never be satisfied to give up, and then later on feel that we might have found them if we'd only kept out another mile or two."

"My sentiments, exactly," declared Will, who possessed a tender heart, as his chums knew from experience.

So the time crept on.

Frank was bending above the motor, but all the while he kept one eye over his shoulder on the bow of the boat where his chum stood, still sweeping the sea ahead with the marine glasses.

In fact, every one aboard seemed to have his gaze focussed on

Jerry by this time, as though he might be the one to decide whether the hunt had better be abandoned right then and there, or kept up still longer.

And Frank almost held his breath awaiting the verdict.

Suddenly he saw Jerry start, and screw the glasses more eagerly to his eyes, as he craned his neck to see the better. With the increasing wind the waves had commenced to rise a little, consequently any floating object might at times be difficult to discern.

"I had a glimpse of something then, fellows! But, after all, it might have been another bunch of old pelicans!" he exclaimed.

"Not that. Pelicans would not be so far out. They hug pretty close to the shore, where the water is more shallow, and the fish come in to feed. Still, it may have been the fin of a shark cutting the water like that one - " started Frank, when Jerry interrupted him:

"There it is again! As sure as you live, I believe it's a man clinging to some sort of wreckage! Here, take the glasses, Frank! Right over there, dead ahead! Now be ready! There! See?"

"It *is* a man! Yes - two of them! Fellows, we are in time!" cried Frank.

"Hurrah!" the others shouted in chorus.

And the breeze, coming off shore, must have carried that volume of cheering sound to the ears of the almost despairing balloonists as they clung there to the wreck of their disabled air craft, possibly arranged to float for a time if it dropped into the sea.

"Yes. There! I can see one of them waving his hand! Give the poor chaps another shout, boys! This is great luck for us!"

exclaimed Frank, and his own sturdy voice helped to swell the sound that rolled over the water.

If it was a happy moment for the rescuers, imagine the feelings of the two who clung there, expecting that every minute might see them without any support, as the waterlogged balloon sank under them!

Fast though the motor-boat was shooting through the waves, she seemed to fairly crawl, such was the impatience of the young voyagers.

So they swept alongside the floating balloonists. When Professor Smythe discovered the identity of those who were coming to his aid his astonishment knew no bounds. It was the most remarkable coincidence he could remember meeting with in an adventurous career extending over many years.

"Was that your camp we passed over, a little while back?" he asked, as, having been helped aboard, and some instruments being passed up by his assistant, he helped the latter to crawl over the gunwale of the motor-boat.

"Just what it was," laughed Frank, "and you came near wrecking us, too. The sand bag struck the tent, and carried it down in a heap."

"Incredible! And yet that very fact goes to prove my assertion that in war time dynamite could be easily dropped into a fortress by means of a dirigible balloon, or an aeroplane. That was a happy thought of mine to send a message. Only I hope none of you brave boys received any injury!" cried the professor.

"Luckily not. But what is to be done with this wreckage?" asked Frank.

"Nothing. It will sink presently. We have secured all our valuable instruments and records. I'm only too happy over escaping from a watery grave. Simms and myself were making up our minds that our time had come when you hove in sight."

"We are heading for Cedar Keys, but in no hurry to get there, professor. What would you like us to do for you?" asked Frank presently, after they had given both men blankets to throw about their shoulders, for the air was "nippy."

"There is smoke on the horizon, to the west I believe it must be a steamer bound for Tampa. Do you think it would be possible to intercept her and put us aboard?" asked the scientist eagerly.

Frank took a look at the weather.

"We'll make a try, anyhow. But to do so we must head straight out, for she will go miles to the south of us," he said.

They sped on for an hour. The land was dim in the distance. It thrilled them to know they were like a speck out in the midst of the great Gulf of Mexico. By now the coast steamer was in plain view, and signals were made for her to stop.

When the captain learned who the two men were, and that he could further the work of the government, he gladly took them aboard; and the last the boys saw of the aeronauts was their waving hats as the steamer went on her way.

CHAPTER XXIV

THE "NORTHER"

"Is it back to the shore now, Frank?"

"If we are wise we'll lose no time in heading that way," was the quick response.

"What's the matter? Is there anything wrong?" demanded Jerry, taking the alarm immediately from his chum's manner.

"I think we are in for another little experience. If you notice, there are clouds along the horizon. I imagine our long-delayed norther is about to swoop down on us before long."

"Talk to me about the tough luck 'of that, will you! Of all times, that it should pick out this to tackle us!" exclaimed Jerry.

He had seen the dark clouds Frank mentioned, and noted that the wind was no longer in the east, but had swung around to the southwest almost magically.

Of course, they were making as fast time as the motor-boat could boast toward the dim shore line. How very far away it seemed to be! Will turned a little white as he contemplated the coming storm catching the small boat out upon the broad bosom of the great gulf.

In doing an errand of mercy they had unconsciously put their heads in the lion's mouth.

Those were very anxious minutes for the chums. Each throb of the motor was taking them closer to the land, but the clouds were rising, and the wind increasing, all too fast to please Frank.

When they were about two miles off shore he commenced to scan the scene before them with renewed eagerness. Much depended upon whether they would have the good luck to strike in at a place where shelter might be found against the fury of the storm when the waves assumed giant proportions.

The gallant little boat behaved splendidly, although there were times when it seemed to Will that his heart jumped into his throat with agony as he imagined that the whirling propeller, exposed to view by the rapid sweep of a billow, might be twisted from its shaft, and ruin come upon them.

And the little dinghy floated astern like a duck, riding the rollers with ease. Again was that valuable glass brought into use, this time searching for a haven, rather than to discover lost balloonists.

"Frank," said Jerry presently, "let me take the wheel while you look through the glasses here. I believe I sighted a key just over yonder, where you see that high palmetto. It seems closer than others just behind."

One look Frank gave.

"Boys, there's a chance for us!" he cried, "for that is certainly an island, and if there only happens to be deep water back of it we can make a harbor."

"Then you're going to risk it?" demanded Bluff.

"There's nothing else to be done. If we head straight on we

must go ashore perhaps half a mile from the land itself. If we try to run down the coast we will be capsized, because we present our broadside to the seas, and they're getting worse and worse every minute," declared Frank firmly.

"Frank is right. It is our only hope," said Jerry.

There were some white faces in the little anxious group as the motor-boat swept resistlessly onward. If all went well, they would find shelter behind the friendly key before many minutes. Should it shoal up rapidly, they must be hopelessly wrecked, and perhaps drowned, in the whirl of foamy water.

The sky was by this time covered with black clouds, and the wind increasing to almost hurricane force. Frank knew that they were sweeping onward at more than twenty miles an hour. Once they struck a reef, while going at this pace, and it meant an end to Cousin Archie's pretty boat, and imminent peril concerning themselves.

Now he could see that he had made no mistake about the key. They swept around the northern end of the jutting land, and Jerry, who was clinging in the bow, trying to gain new confidence by thrusting the pole downward from time to time, kept on announcing that he could not strike bottom.

Gradually Frank steered in such fashion that they gained the protection of a point. Then the boys broke out into a shout that voiced their sentiments of thanksgiving at an almost miraculous escape.

It was not difficult to find a snug harbor after that. Of course, the norther was soon in full swing, it being really the first genuine experience our cruisers had met with in that line.

The air grew very cold, and they were glad to get ashore and build a roaring fire in a sheltered spot. Indeed, it was speedily determined that they would hug that same cheery blaze as long as the visitor from the frigid North remained.

Heavy rain had accompanied the first of the storm, but this soon ceased, and a steady roar of wind through the palmettos sounded like a railroad train passing over a long trestle. The waves breaking on the north end of the sand key also added to the wild clamor.

All that day and the next they were stormbound. Of course, Jerry could not be kept idle. Fishing was out of the question during such a blow, but he discovered that there was plenty of game to be had with Frank's shotgun. Ducks could be obtained in any number, such as they were. Frank tried skinning them to get rid of the fishy flavor, and found it answered splendidly. Coots, treated in the same way, afforded a very palatable stew.

Then on the mainland, where Jerry managed to go by aid of the dinghy, he was lucky enough to stir up several bevy of quail, from which he took fair toll.

Meanwhile Bluff, seized with a sudden sense of his duties as the owner of a repeating shotgun, hied him away along the protected inner shore of the key, and managed to gather in a full dozen snipe and shore birds of various species, some of which proved to be very delicious.

So they passed the time away, making merry, as care-free lads will. Often Frank and Jerry talked mysteriously together, while little Joe was busily engaged about the fire. Undoubtedly the two good-hearted boys were trying to hatch up some sort of scheme whereby the youngster might be benefited.

On the third day they determined to start out. The sea had gone down to decent proportions, with a promise of several fair days ahead, as is always the case after a norther has cleared the atmosphere. Besides, their time was nearing an end, and they must get closer to Cedar Keys.

A long day's run was taken, and as they sought a snug harbor that afternoon the solemn face of Frank assured his chums that they were near the end of their delightful winter vacation.

"If you look over yonder, fellows," said Frank as they drifted slowly toward the harbor that had been selected for the night's anchorage, "you'll see something that will tell you the city on the key is close at hand. To-morrow we will wind up our little cruise, I'm sorry to say."

A groan greeted this announcement, although they had suspected that such an ending to their happy time was imminent.

Jerry reluctantly raised the marine glasses.

"Yes, it's a fact, fellows," he said slowly. "I can see the wharves and some of the boats, as well as church steeples. That's Cedar Keys, all right."

"Then this is our last night in camp. Well, boys, don't let's get the blues. We've had a bully good time, and will never forget what has come our way. Why, the rescuing of the wrecked balloonists alone paid us for coming," said Will.

They found plenty of water, and anchored in the mouth of the famous Suwanee River, with the busy city something like twelve miles away.

Once more they went ashore, and on the bank of the stream of which they had so many times sung they built their last campfire and put up their tent.

"Lucky we bundled those things in before leaving that camp, when searching for the lost balloonists," said Will, who was figuring on getting a picture of the scene in the morning, to finish up his series.

"Yes, for otherwise we'd have had to sleep on board to-night," laughed Frank.

Supper over, they sat around, talking and laughing, in the endeavor to forget the sorrow that gnawed at their boyish hearts. They had enjoyed this trip so much that it would be with the keenest regret that they turned their backs on the Sunny South, and once more struck out for the snow-clad hills of their native land.

Jerry sang, and Bluff orated to his heart's content. Finally they noticed that Frank was looking at something he held in his hand.

"It's the sealed document his father gave him before starting," said Bluff.

"Tell me about that, will you! Frank, didn't he give you permission to open it when you came in sight of Cedar Keys?" cried Jerry eagerly.

Frank, in reply, was tearing off the end of the envelope, a smile of expectation on his face.

"I guess it's going to turn out a joke," hazarded Bluff.

"Now, I've been thinking that perhaps they settled it we should come up by way of the ocean from Jacksonville," declared Will, "and that's the surprise."

"How is it, Frank? Tell us about it!" cried Jerry as he saw the face of the other light up when his eyes took in the import of the communication he found inside the envelope his father had given him.

Frank turned around. His gaze did not rest immediately on his chums, but was given entirely to little Joe, which fact amazed the others still more.

"It's the greatest thing ever, fellows! It makes me so happy I hardly know whether I'm dreaming or not! And the best of it is, the whole business is about our little campmate here,

Joe Abercrombie!" was what he said, seizing the lad's hand
warmly.

CHAPTER XXV

THE SECRET OF THE SEALED PACKET - CONCLUSION

"About me!" exclaimed Joe, looking amazed.

"Talk to me about surprises!" ejaculated Jerry. "Frank does love to knock us all silly!"

"How could your father know about Joe, here?" demanded skeptical Lawyer Bluff.

"Joe, what was your father's name?" asked Frank, eagerness in his bright eyes.

"Joseph Sprague Abercrombie," came the immediate response.

"Hurrah! That settles it!" shouted Frank, throwing his hat into the air. His chums could not ever remember having seen him one-half so excited before.

"Take pity on us!" cried Will, catching the other by the sleeve.

"Yes, hurry up and tell, or I'll burst!" ejaculated Bluff.

Jerry shook Frank, in his earnestness, saying:

"It isn't fair, and you know it! We're chums, and we deserve to be taken into your confidence."

"Right you are; and now sit down and listen to me. I'm not going to read this letter out, but you can look it over later, as you please. My father says he was just about to come down to Cedar Keys himself, or send a trusted clerk, for the business is very important, you see."

"And that was why he smiled when you told him where we meant to bring up?"

"Yes, Bluff, that was the reason. Now you know he is a banker and a capitalist. In times gone by he used to be in Wall Street, so he had connection with many men who were investors. One friend of his, named Joseph Sprague Abercrombie, who was an engineer, entrusted some money to him to invest in certain stocks. By an unfortunate turn of the market those stocks became seemingly valueless. They have lain in his safe for ten years."

"Say! it's growing exciting! I can see what's coming!" cried Bluff.

"Meanwhile, my father had lost all track of his once boyhood friend Joe. Then, by a strange freak of fate, the corporation that had issued those stocks suddenly became alive. Everything they owned began to prosper. Their mines turned out rich investments, their timber lands found a big market. The apparently worthless stock, taken from the safe and put on the market at its highest point, brought in a fortune for Joseph Abercrombie or his heirs!"

"Hurrah!" shouted Will, embracing little Joe in the exuberance of his joy.

"Talk to me about magic, will you! This thing has the Arabian Nights beaten all to a frazzle, and that's what I think!" laughed Jerry, pumping the hand of Joe vigorously.

"My father tried hard to locate his old friend. By degrees he found that he had gone South, soon after sinking his little savings in what seemed to have been worthless stock. Then he learned that he had lost his life on the road, and that his family with but scant means, had moved to Cedar Keys, where they were still living, according to what information he could secure."

"It's great, that's what! And to think that we should have run across Joe here in such a marvelous way!" said Bluff.

"Yes," spoke up the lad quickly, "and I believe you saved my life, too. I'd been killed by them men, my uncle with the rest; or else I'd tried to escape, and might 'a' lost myself ashore, to died in the swamps. I'll never forget it, never!"

After all, that evening was by long odds the happiest of the whole trip. They sat around the fire until long after midnight. Indeed, it was hard to get any one to admit that he was sleepy in the least degree.

"Our last camp, fellows. Perhaps we may never be able to all meet under canvas again," said Jerry as they finally set about seeking their beds.

If Jerry could have lifted the curtain of the future a bit he would never have ventured that doleful prophecy. There were other camps in store for the four outdoor chums, many of them, and in a country whither their longing souls had often turned - the wilderness around the great Rockies. But it is not our province to mention any of the wonderful adventures that were fated to befall them there. All those things will be duly set down in the next volume of this series, which will be called: "The Outdoor Chums After Big Game; or, Perilous Adventures in the Wilderness."

When breakfast had been dispatched in the morning, for the last time the four outdoor chums took down the dear old khaki tent and folded it away reverently. They looked upon it as a friend and comforter indeed.

Then they went aboard the *Jessamine*, and started for the city, which could be seen upon the key, over the gleaming, sun-kissed water of the gulf.

They arrived long before noon, and leaving the boat in the hands of the party to whom Frank bore a letter from his cousin, the four chums accompanied little Joe to his modest home.

Here the delightful news was broken to the widow of Mr. Langdon's old boyhood friend. Words would be useless to describe her joy. The clouds had rolled away as if by magic, and at last she could see a happy future for herself and her family, marred by only one keen regret, and that the absence of the brave man who had died at his post years before.

Our boys spent a couple of days in Cedar Keys. Letters were found there from the home folks. At last they started north once more, to resume their school duties, satisfied that they had enjoyed the finest vacation in all their experience.

Their work in saving the lost balloonists was spoken of in the papers, for the professor would never forget what he owed them. He even took pains to write to Mr. Langdon and praise the conduct of the boys.

Safely landed again in Centerville, and once more taking up their school work, we shall have to part from the boys.

"Well, it was a great outing!" declared Will.

"Talk to me about good times!" came from Jerry. "We never had a better."

"Right you are," added Frank. "And the photos are all dandy."

"They'll certainly be fine, to keep and look over in years to come," remarked Will.

And here we will take leave of the Outdoor Chums and say good-by.

Choose from Thousands of 1stWorldLibrary Classics By

A. M. Barnard
Ada Leverson
Adolphus William Ward
Aesop
Agatha Christie
Alexander Aaronsohn
Alexander Kielland
Alexandre Dumas
Alfred Gatty
Alfred Ollivant
Alice Duer Miller
Alice Turner Curtis
Alice Dunbar
Allen Chapman
Ambrose Bierce
Amelia E. Barr
Amory H. Bradford
Andrew Lang
Andrew McFarland Davis
Andy Adams
Anna Alice Chapin
Anna Sewell
Annie Besant
Annie Hamilton Donnell
Annie Payson Call
Annie Roe Carr
Annonaymous
Anton Chekhov
Arnold Bennett
Arthur Conan Doyle
Arthur M. Winfield
Arthur Ransome
Arthur Schnitzler
Atticus
B.H. Baden-Powell
B. M. Bower
B. C. Chatterjee
Baroness Emmuska Orczy
Baroness Orczy
Basil King
Bayard Taylor
Ben Macomber
Bertha Muzzy Bower
Bjornstjerne Bjornson
Booth Tarkington
Boyd Cable
Bram Stoker
C. Collodi
C. E. Orr

C. M. Ingleby
Carolyn Wells
Catherine Parr Traill
Charles A. Eastman
Charles Amory Beach
Charles Dickens
Charles Dudley Warner
Charles Farrar Browne
Charles Ives
Charles Kingsley
Charles Klein
Charles Hanson Towne
Charles Lathrop Pack
Charles Romyn Dake
Charles Whibley
Charles Willing Beale
Charlotte M. Braeme
Charlotte M. Yonge
Charlotte Perkins Stetson
Clair W. Hayes
Clarence Day Jr.
Clarence E. Mulford
Clemence Housman
Confucius
Coningsby Dawson
Cornelis DeWitt Wilcox
Cyril Burleigh
D. H. Lawrence
Daniel Defoe
David Garnett
Dinah Craik
Don Carlos Janes
Donald Keyhoe
Dorothy Kilner
Dougan Clark
Douglas Fairbanks
E. Nesbit
E.P.Roe
E. Phillips Oppenheim
Earl Barnes
Edgar Rice Burroughs
Edith Van Dyne
Edith Wharton
Edward Everett Hale
Edward J. O'Biren
Edward S. Ellis
Edwin L. Arnold
Eleanor Atkins
Eliot Gregory

Elizabeth Gaskell
Elizabeth McCracken
Elizabeth Von Arnim
Ellem Key
Emerson Hough
Emilie F. Carlen
Emily Dickinson
Enid Bagnold
Enilor Macartney Lane
Erasmus W. Jones
Ernie Howard Pie
Ethel May Dell
Ethel Turner
Ethel Watts Mumford
Eugenie Foa
Eugene Wood
Eustace Hale Ball
Evelyn Everett-green
Everard Cotes
F. H. Cheley
F. J. Cross
F. Marion Crawford
Federick Austin Ogg
Ferdinand Ossendowski
Francis Bacon
Francis Darwin
Frances Hodgson Burnett
Frances Parkinson Keyes
Frank Gee Patchin
Frank Harris
Frank Jewett Mather
Frank L. Packard
Frank V. Webster
Frederic Stewart Isham
Frederick Trevor Hill
Frederick Winslow Taylor
Friedrich Kerst
Friedrich Nietzsche
Fyodor Dostoyevsky
G.A. Henty
G.K. Chesterton
Gabrielle E. Jackson
Garrett P. Serviss
Gaston Leroux
George A. Warren
George Ade
Geroge Bernard Shaw
George Durston
George Ebers

George Eliot
George Gissing
George MacDonald
George Meredith
George Orwell
George Sylvester Viereck
George Tucker
George W. Cable
George Wharton James
Gertrude Atherton
Gordon Casserly
Grace E. King
Grace Gallatin
Grace Greenwood
Grant Allen
Guillermo A. Sherwell
Gulielma Zollinger
Gustav Flaubert
H. A. Cody
H. B. Irving
H.C. Bailey
H. G. Wells
H. H. Munro
H. Irving Hancock
H. Rider Haggard
H. W. C. Davis
Haldeman Julius
Hall Caine
Hamilton Wright Mabie
Hans Christian Andersen
Harold Avery
Harold McGrath
Harriet Beecher Stowe
Harry Castlemon
Harry Coghill
Harry Houidini
Hayden Carruth
Helent Hunt Jackson
Helen Nicolay
Hendrik Conscience
Hendy David Thoreau
Henri Barbusse
Henrik Ibsen
Henry Adams
Henry Ford
Henry Frost
Henry James
Henry Jones Ford
Henry Seton Merriman
Henry W Longfellow
Herbert A. Giles

Herbert Carter
Herbert N. Casson
Herman Hesse
Hildegard G. Frey
Homer
Honore De Balzac
Horace B. Day
Horace Walpole
Horatio Alger Jr.
Howard Pyle
Howard R. Garis
Hugh Lofting
Hugh Walpole
Humphry Ward
Ian Maclaren
Inez Haynes Gillmore
Irving Bacheller
Isabel Hornibrook
Israel Abrahams
Ivan Turgenev
J.G.Austin
J. Henri Fabre
J. M. Barrie
J. Macdonald Oxley
J. S. Fletcher
J. S. Knowles
J. Storer Clouston
Jack London
Jacob Abbott
James Allen
James Andrews
James Baldwin
James Branch Cabell
James DeMille
James Joyce
James Lane Allen
James Lane Allen
James Oliver Curwood
James Oppenheim
James Otis
James R. Driscoll
Jane Austen
Jane L. Stewart
Janet Aldridge
Jens Peter Jacobsen
Jerome K. Jerome
John Burroughs
John Cournos
John F. Kennedy
John Gay
John Glasworthy

John Habberton
John Joy Bell
John Kendrick Bangs
John Milton
John Philip Sousa
Jonas Lauritz Idemil Lie
Jonathan Swift
Joseph A. Altsheler
Joseph Carey
Joseph Conrad
Joseph E. Badger Jr
Joseph Hergesheimer
Joseph Jacobs
Jules Vernes
Julian Hawthrone
Julie A Lippmann
Justin Huntly McCarthy
Kakuzo Okakura
Kenneth Grahame
Kenneth McGaffey
Kate Langley Bosher
Kate Langley Bosher
Katherine Cecil Thurston
Katherine Stokes
L. A. Abbot
L. T. Meade
L. Frank Baum
Latta Griswold
Laura Dent Crane
Laura Lee Hope
Laurence Housman
Lawrence Beasley
Leo Tolstoy
Leonid Andreyev
Lewis Carroll
Lewis Sperry Chafer
Lilian Bell
Lloyd Osbourne
Louis Hughes
Louis Tracy
Louisa May Alcott
Lucy Fitch Perkins
Lucy Maud Montgomery
Luther Benson
Lydia Miller Middleton
Lyndon Orr
M. Corvus
M. H. Adams
Margaret E. Sangster
Margret Howth
Margaret Vandercook

Margret Penrose
Maria Edgeworth
Maria Thompson Daviess
Mariano Azuela
Marion Polk Angellotti
Mark Overton
Mark Twain
Mary Austin
Mary Catherine Crowley
Mary Cole
Mary Hastings Bradley
Mary Roberts Rinehart
Mary Rowlandson
M. Wollstonecraft Shelley
Maud Lindsay
Max Beerbohm
Myra Kelly
Nathaniel Hawthrone
Nicolo Machiavelli
O. F. Walton
Oscar Wilde
Owen Johnson
P.G. Wodehouse
Paul and Mabel Thorne
Paul G. Tomlinson
Paul Severing
Percy Brebner
Peter B. Kyne
Plato
R. Derby Holmes
R. L. Stevenson
R. S. Ball
Rabindranath Tagore
Rahul Alvares
Ralph Bonehill
Ralph Henry Barbour
Ralph Victor
Ralph Waldo Emmerson
Rene Descartes
Rex Beach

Rex E. Beach
Richard Harding Davis
Richard Jefferies
Richard Le Gallienne
Robert Barr
Robert Frost
Robert Gordon Anderson
Robert L. Drake
Robert Lansing
Robert Lynd
Robert Michael Ballantyne
Robert W. Chambers
Rosa Nouchette Carey
Rudyard Kipling
Samuel B. Allison
Samuel Hopkins Adams
Sarah Bernhardt
Sarah C. Hallowell
Selma Lagerlof
Sherwood Anderson
Sigmund Freud
Standish O'Grady
Stanley Weyman
Stella Benson
Stella M. Francis
Stephen Crane
Stewart Edward White
Stijn Streuvels
Swami Abhedananda
Swami Parmananda
T. S. Ackland
T. S. Arthur
The Princess Der Ling
Thomas A. Janvier
Thomas A Kempis
Thomas Anderton
Thomas Bailey Aldrich
Thomas Bulfinch
Thomas De Quincey
Thomas Dixon

Thomas H. Huxley
Thomas Hardy
Thomas More
Thornton W. Burgess
U. S. Grant
Valentine Williams
Various Authors
Vaughan Kester
Victor Appleton
Victoria Cross
Virginia Woolf
Wadsworth Camp
Walter Camp
Walter Scott
Washington Irving
Wilbur Lawton
Wilkie Collins
Willa Cather
Willard F. Baker
William Dean Howells
William le Queux
W. Makepeace Thackeray
William W. Walter
William Shakespeare
Winston Churchill
Yei Theodora Ozaki
Yogi Ramacharaka
Young E. Allison
Zane Grey

www.ingramcontent.com/pod-product-compliance
Lightning Source LLC
Chambersburg PA
CBHW020503100426
42813CB00030B/3094/J